Not Just Milk Stout

Not Just Milk Stout

The Mackeson Family and Their Hythe Brewery

Anne Petrie

The History Press

First published 2023

The History Press
97 St George's Place, Cheltenham,
Gloucestershire, GL50 3QB
www.thehistorypress.co.uk

British Library Cataloguing in Publication Data.
A catalogue record for this book is available from the British Library.

ISBN 978 1 80399 457 4

Typesetting and origination by The History Press.
Printed and bound in Great Britain by TJ Books Limited, Padstow, Cornwall.

MIX
Paper from responsible sources
FSC www.fsc.org FSC® C013056

Trees for Life

CONTENTS

ACKNOWLEDGEMENTS

My thanks are due to my fellow members of Hythe Local History Group, especially Mike de la Mare, Ron Greenwood, Iris Pearce and Paul Naylor for reading the text and helping with the photographs. Kevin Bailey, the curator of Hythe Museum, showed me some lovely breweriana and Peter Henderson, the archivist of the King's School, Canterbury, went far beyond my original enquiry about admission records. Robert Melrose lent me the diaries of General Frederick Solly-Flood, which helped put Hythe society into perspective.

I also received much-appreciated help and advice from Daniel Korachi-Alaoui at Canterbury Cathedral Archives; from Rachel Lang of University College London Centre for the Study of the Legacies of British Slavery; and from Duncan Sambrook of Sambrook's Brewery in London and his colleague, brewer John Hatch. Staff at Kent History and Library Centre, at the British Library and at Hythe Library could not have been more helpful.

All these people kindly shared the knowledge and expertise that I lacked and I cannot thank them enough. I must also express my gratitude to those who have allowed me to use their photographs as illustrations: Anne Thompson; the Rev. Michael Darkins of St Leonard's church, Hythe; and Hythe Civic Society.

Note on Mackeson Names

The Mackeson family produced four generations of first sons called Henry. To avoid confusion, I have adopted the following stratagem:

Henry Mackeson of Deal (1737–1800) is just 'Henry';
Henry Mackeson, his son (1772–1860), the first brewery owner, is 'Harry';
Henry Bean Mackeson, Harry's son (1813–94), is 'Henry Bean';
Henry Mackeson, Henry Bean's son (1861–1935), is 'Young Henry',

All these men were actually known as 'Harry' to their families and Young Henry finally christened his first born just that: Harry Ripley Mackeson (1905–64).

PROLOGUE

On an otherwise unremarkable Monday in October 1801, two young men sat down in a room in Hythe with three others, rather older. Two copies of a large document, an indenture on vellum, were produced and carefully read before being signed by three of the men and witnessed by the other two.

The younger pair were Harry and William Mackeson, brothers, originally from Deal, but now living in Hythe and, since the document had been signed, the owners of the town's brewery and several inns. Of the others, one was their late mother's great-uncle, John Friend, the erstwhile owner of the brewery, whose Mackeson kinsmen had just agreed to pay him, albeit in instalments, £11,469. To put this in context, the average family income in 1801 was £92 a year.[1] The witnesses were brothers, too, members of the Tournay family. Both were attorneys at law. This was a serious matter, worthy of the attention of serious men.

Neither Mackeson brother had planned to become a brewer and both had started out on different career paths, but this simple, if rather expensive, transaction transformed their lives, the lives of their families and the town of Hythe.

In the eighteenth century, nearly every town in the country, large or small, had its brewery. Few survived, as the Mackeson brewery did, into the second half of the twentieth century and few had a product that became a household name. Mackeson Milk Stout was from 1909 the Hythe brewery's unique selling point, widely advertised as being both healthy and appropriate for women to drink at home or in company. Milk stout even found its way into one of the nation's favourite soaps, *Coronation Street*.

The success of their venture made the Mackeson brothers and their descendants well-off by small town standards. They could afford to educate their children and support their careers and vocations away from the brewery, which after all was still 'trade' and therefore not quite respectable. The family produced physicians, generals, lawyers, priests and admirals and finally, in the person of Brigadier Sir Harry Ripley Mackeson, a Lord of the Treasury and a baronet. That he was also the MP for Hythe is indicative of the strong links the family had with the town.

Hythe in 1801 was a quiet little place, long past its glory days as an original member of the Cinque Ports confederation, when, with the monarch's blessing, its citizens made a fortune out of legalised piracy on the high seas. Incorporated by royal charter, it still had the right to return two MPs to Parliament though it now had a population of only a little over 1,000. It was small, even by small town standards in a country with a population of less than 9 million, comprising just 200 householders and their families, offspring, lodgers, apprentices, servants and journeymen.[2] It was a young town, too: nearly 40 per cent of the population was under 15, a trend reflected in England as a whole. There was a charity school for poor children, an 'Academy' run by William Card for the sons of the middling sort, or the King's School in Canterbury, for those who could afford the fees. The over-60s were less in evidence, but there was some provision for the indigent elderly in the form of two almshouses, St John's and St Bartholomew's.

The usual trades were represented in the town: butchers, shoemakers, millers, tailors, drapers, coal merchants, carpenters, bricklayers, grocers, a basket maker, a weaver, a baker and a blacksmith. There was a tannery situated at the east end of the town, allowing its stink to be swept by the prevailing south-westerly winds toward Folkestone. There were also more unusual trades, like that of James Hyam, a peruke maker. Thanks to the Duty on Hair Powder Act of 1795, the golden age of wig-wearing was fading but Hythe was not at the cutting edge of fashion. There was a collar maker, not for men's shirts, which still had soft necklines, but for horses and given that there were seventy-eight draught horses in the town, Robert Bowen was likely to have been busy. John Raisbeck was a brazier or brass worker producing buttons, buckles, door furniture, fire grates and candlesticks.

Then there were the men who were employed to fight organised crime – smuggling or 'free trade' as its practitioners preferred to call it. John Manning and Henry 'One-Eyed' Tritton were Customs Riding Officers, paid a pittance to patrol the coast and gather intelligence. They reported to the Customs Supervisor, Isaac Tournay, a brother to the witnesses of the Mackesons' purchase of the brewery.

Reflecting Hythe's rural hinterland, there were farmers and graziers, owning between them nearly 700 sheep. The fleeces these produced were dealt with by the appropriately named Thomas Woolley, a wool stapler.

The town also had a few men who did not get their hands dirty, 'gentry' as the directories called them, though the term was not definitive. Most 'gentry' in Hythe would have been regarded as country bumpkins in London. Perhaps an exception was William Deedes, owner of the Old Manor House in the town, a Deputy Lieutenant of Kent, Lieutenant Colonel commandant of the South Kent Volunteers and relation by marriage of Jane Austen. He, however, was in the process of leaving Hythe for a much grander house up the hill, Sandling Park, designed by Joseph Bonomi the Elder.

At the other end of the social scale, most of the other male residents of the town who were not tradesmen would have been unskilled labourers.

The brewery stood at the western end of the High Street, which was of beaten earth and unlit at night. The houses lining the street were mostly old, with none of the elegant Regency terraces of Brighton or Bath, though some householders had covered their timbered frontages with brick, complete with what we now recognise as typically Georgian windows and doors. Pigs, goats and chickens roamed the streets, despite the town corporation's endless attempts to compel their owners to keep them penned.

There was a small Thursday stock market and a general market on Saturdays, held under the town hall, which was quite new, built in 1794. John Friend had given some of the land on which it was built.[3] It served as a courtroom as well as a meeting place for jurats (town councillors). While they awaited trial, the accused were kept in the town gaol, more or less voluntarily since it was laughably easy to escape from it. There was also an annual fair, held on the town green, each November.

There was only one church, St Leonard's, up the hill from the town and once the pride of the Cinque Port but now rather shabby, though it had a new tower, built in 1750 to replace one that had collapsed eleven years earlier. St Leonard's was not a parish church, but a chapel of ease, Hythe forming part of the parish of Saltwood, a mile or so up the hill. Nonconformists and Roman Catholics had to wait a while before they could worship without travelling some distance.

Travel was difficult, as it was throughout the country, although the profits from turnpikes were being used to improve roads. There had been a toll road to Ashford from Hythe since 1762, though the road to Canterbury, Stone Street, was not turnpiked and was described as 'very rough'.[4] For travel further afield, for those who could not afford a carriage or horse hire, there was a thrice-weekly coach service to London, which returned overnight.[5]

If heavy loads needed to be transported, the easiest method was by sea. Although Hythe was one of the original Cinque Ports, its haven, always subject to silting, had finally succumbed to the longshore drift of the shingle in the late seventeenth century. Now, boats anchored off Hythe and the loads were hauled up the beach by means of a winch turned by wretched 'sea horses'. Coal was delivered to the town in this way well into the nineteenth century. For less bulky loads, or for passengers who could not face the rigours of a road journey, there were regular hoys plying between Hythe and Griffin's wharf, almost opposite the Tower of London.[6]

The shingle that had clogged up Hythe haven was gradually drained – 'inned' – and was by the time the Mackesons arrived in town used for grazing land. This flat terrain continued westwards for 25 miles, across the Romney Marsh, sparsely populated except for its small towns, Lydd and New Romney, both also former ports now stranded inland. To the east of Hythe lay hillier land and the towns of Folkestone and Dover, and to the north was the village of Saltwood and the chalk escarpment of the North Downs.

It is fair to say that not a lot happened in Hythe. A glance at the newspapers in the year before the Mackesons' arrival shows that the only newsworthy events, apart from births, deaths, marriages and a mayor-making, were the disappearance of a brown horse from a field near the turnpike and the illicit slaying of a fat sheep.

THE FAMILY OF HENRY MACKESON

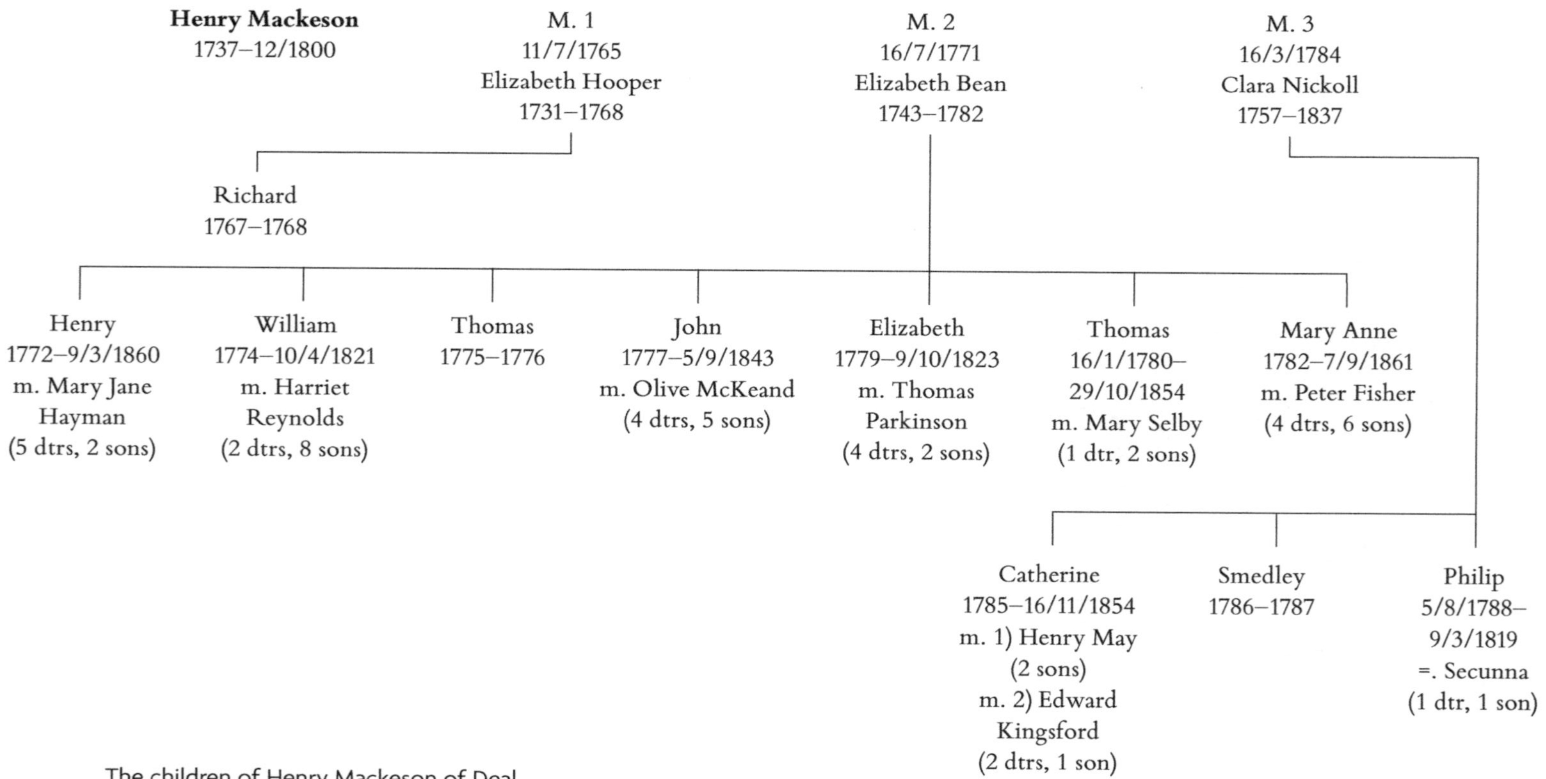

The children of Henry Mackeson of Deal.

1

A VERY NICE BEGINNING

Harry and William (known to the family as Will) were the eldest sons of Henry Mackeson, born just fourteen months apart in 1772 and 1774 respectively. Their childhood was spent in Deal, about 20 miles along the coast from Hythe.

Their father was a mariner who in 1765 had married a widow, Elizabeth Hooper. She had inherited from her first husband a large house in Middle Street, Deal. She gave birth to a son in 1767, but the next year she and the infant died. Though she left the house in trust to her two sons by her first marriage, Henry Mackeson bought it from the estate and continued to live there after his second marriage, in 1771, to Elizabeth Bean of nearby Great Mongeham. She became the mother of Harry and Will and, importantly, as it would turn out, was the great-niece of John Friend, Ashford maltster and Hythe brewer.[1]

In July 1779, Henry Mackeson was appointed by James Boxer of Folkestone to be first lieutenant on board one of his ships. This was no ordinary assignment: two days earlier, Boxer had been authorised by the king to crew a privateer to sail against the Spanish in 'a warlike manner' and to seize ships and prizes.[2] England had declared war on Spain in June as a result of its support for the Americans in their War of Independence.

It was probably the profits from this venture that allowed Henry to leave the sea. In 1792 a local directory records him as still living in the Middle Street house, where he had built wine vaults and stables and was trading as a wine merchant.[3]

By this time, his second wife was dead and he had married for a third time, to Clara Nickoll. Together, they produced three children to add to the six Henry had fathered with Elizabeth Bean.

Harry, the eldest son, joined his father in the wine trade. Henry suffered from gout and by the last years of the century Harry was responsible for most of the business.[4] Will, at the age of 14, was apprenticed for seven years to Benjamin Bell, surgeon of Edinburgh.[5] He was fortunate to be taken on by such a distinguished practitioner. Bell, Professor of Surgery and Obstetrics at Edinburgh University, was both a surgical pioneer and a man of science whose renown, thanks to his published works, had spread far beyond Scotland.

His time served, Will went home to Deal and set himself up in Lower Street as a 'Surgeon, Apothecary and Man-midwife'.[6] The man-midwife

George Cruikshank's 1793 satirical cartoon. *The Wellcome Library no. 16968i*

was still a controversial figure in the late eighteenth century and was more fashionable in elite society than among the middle classes of small towns. An anonymous tract, *The Danger and Immodesty of the Present Custom of Unnecessarily Employing Men-Midwives*, was published only twenty years before Will started practising and the occupation was generally regarded as both unmanly and ungentlemanly. One authority tells us that a man-midwife, to compete with female practitioners, needed highly developed social skills and a professional demeanour. He had to be 'sober, patient and discreet, polite and easy in his address and manners'.[7]

Perhaps Deal was not ready for such a novelty or Will, in his early 20s, lacked the necessary social polish. Despite the failure of his venture, he continued to describe himself as a surgeon for some years after he and Harry had acquired the brewery.

Henry Mackeson died in 1800, at lodgings in Canterbury,[8] leaving over £11,000.[9] Just before he died, he had given Harry and Will an advance on their inheritance of £1,600 between them.[10] They and their stepmother Clara were appointed joint executors of Henry's will.[11] Apart from the distribution of cash, £1,000 each for two unmarried daughters had to be invested to provide for their marriage settlements.[12] There was a slight difficulty when one of the daughters of Henry's first wife, Elizabeth Hooper, claimed that the Middle Street house was rightfully hers, but the executors paid her £15 for 'quieting and extinguishing the claim'.[13] The house was eventually sold in 1812, by which time the children were all grown and Clara had gone to live in Lambeth. It had been licensed to sell alcohol when Henry Mackeson ran his wine business there and has continued as licensed premises until the modern day, trading since 1865 under the name the Ship Inn.

Harry and Will put their inheritance to use in buying John Friend's Hythe brewery. They had agreed to pay Friend £3,130 immediately for the brewery itself, the dwelling house next to it, the brewery equipment, stock in hand and two inns, the White Hart and the Red Lion, both in Hythe. The balance was to be paid after seven years, in instalments of £500.[14]

The Ship Inn, Deal.
Author's collection

Their involvement in the concern must have started earlier as they were, by the time they signed the indenture, both living in Hythe and were referred to as brewers. Their early correspondence shows that Harry, at least, was conversant with the business and he had another connection with brewing. In 1785, the Hayman brothers of Deal started a brewery in their licensed premises in Lower Street and less than two years later, Harry married Elizabeth Hayman, daughter of Thomas, one of those brothers. Perhaps his interest was sparked by his knowledge of his father-in-law's business and the decision of John Friend to sell his Hythe brewery was a happy coincidence.

Friend had lived in Hythe with an unmarried cousin, Elizabeth Rammell. He had, as his will shows, intended to leave her the bulk of his considerable estate, but in the event, she died ten months before him, in February 1802. When he died, 'highly respected' in December of that year,[15] the offspring of Henry Mackeson and Elizabeth Bean got the lot, a few individual legacies aside.[16]

These subsidiary legacies alone came to over £10,000; although he had lived modestly with only one servant, Friend was wealthy.[17] He died possessed of seven barns; eight stables; a water mill; eleven houses with their curtilages (the enclosed areas of land adjacent to dwelling houses); twelve gardens; six orchards; and 260 acres of agricultural land and woods. The lands covered a wide area in east Kent.[18] We do not know exactly how much the residue payable to the Mackeson children was, but John (Jack) Mackeson, the third son, wrote gleefully from India, where he was serving with the East India Company:

> Mr Friend died worth a good round sum. My share of his property I mean to be the foundation for making a fortune. I shall immediately have £4000 sent out to this country which added to the £1500 I have already will be a very nice beginning.[19]

Jack's confidence that he would one day be the possessor of a fortune was sadly misplaced.

Now on a financially secure footing, Harry and Will could turn their attention to developing their brewery, though the records and the accounts and the copy letters were always kept by Harry, who seems to have become the dominant partner from the start, although no formal deed of partnership was ever entered into by the brothers.[20] Harry, a methodical man, also kept a reference book explaining legal terms and citing case precedents.[21]

The brothers decided early on to advertise the business as 'established in 1669'. The basis of this claim was that Harry had discovered, among the deeds relating to the brewery, a document that detailed a mortgage taken out by James Pashley, its then owner in that year. He believed this to be the earliest record, but there are others extant showing that James Pashley and his father, another James, were brewers in Hythe from at least 1641.[22] The year '1669', though, has a nice ring to it and enabled them to claim that the business was founded 'during the reign of Charles II' rather than 'just before the Civil War'.

The Mackesons opened their brewery for business on Monday, 19 October 1801, a week after signing the indenture. Harry started a brand-new ledger and, in a firm, clear hand wrote:

> Stock & Sundries for an inventory and evaluation of the Stock in Trade of Messrs. Hy. & Wm. Mackeson late of Deal which they have this day taken from Mr John Friend of Hythe.[23]

They had in stock 252 barrels of beer; malt; hops; four horses; two drays and a cart, plus coals and horse feed. On this first day they supplied beer to the Rose Inn, Dymchurch; to the King's Head, Hythe; and to a Mr Gosbee. Porter was sold to William Howard. And they started a new brewing. Beer was traditionally brewed from October to March, so the timing of their acquisition was ideal. By November 1801 they had seven regular customers, who took weekly deliveries; two months later, this had risen to twelve and in September 1803 there were twenty. One customer ordered only twice a year, but the Mackeson brothers were happy to oblige. He was General (later Sir) John Moore, based just a couple of miles from Hythe, at Shorncliffe.[24]

Moore was appointed colonel of the 52nd Regiment of Foot in 1803 and given permission to train it as a light (mobile) corps. In their green uniforms, the soldiers became a familiar sight in the area. Knighted in 1804, Moore was later sent to Portugal and Spain to support resistance to the French there. He was killed at the Battle of Corunna in 1809 and overnight became a national hero.

The brewery the Mackesons had bought was small. It brewed twice a week, with each brew producing about thirty-eight barrels.[25] A barrel contained 36 gallons. By contrast, the London breweries were producing huge quantities: Barclay Perkins in 1815 made almost 30,000 gallons *a day.*[26] Given that the English had a liking for beer – the annual per capita consumption was reckoned to be 33 gallons in 1800[27] – there was scope for expansion, though the brothers could never hope to emulate the huge London breweries, which produced nearly half of the country's beer.

The memorial to Sir John Moore at Sandgate, near Hythe. *Anne Thompson*

Having bought some more land in Hythe, Harry and Will started building – and spending. To finance some of the work, they sold land in Lympne for £2,000.[28] Their cash flow was also helped by rental income of £456 a year,[29] but even so, in May 1803 Harry wrote, 'We are now to expend so large a sum in building that for a considerable time to come we shall be rather short of cash'.[30] Some construction materials were shipped from London and landed on Hythe beach, 'The bricks are all landed safe and I think they will answer extremely well. We were obliged to unload them in the night on account of the tide.'[31]

Given the difficulties of landing goods in Hythe, Harry and Will were attracted by plans to build a proper anchorage in Folkestone. In 1804 Lord Radnor, the little fishing town's predominant landowner, petitioned Parliament for permission to build a stone harbour, and an Act of Parliament was granted in 1807, partly to provide potential anchorages for warships during the Napoleonic Wars and partly because Parliament was then generally sympathetic to the aspirations of merchants and manufacturers. Harry and Will immediately bought shares in the new Folkestone Harbour Company.[32]

Plans drawn up at this time were considered too expensive to implement in full, but civil engineer William Jessop, together with a team that included Thomas Telford, designed and built a western pier that was completed in 1810, followed by another, running at right angles, completed in 1820. Together these drystone walls, which can still be seen today, provided some shelter from the prevailing winds, but it was not until the arrival of the railway in 1843 that a functional harbour was built.

As well as running a business, the brothers had other commitments. In 1793 at Dover Castle, the Lord Warden of the Cinque Ports and the Prime Minister, William Pitt, had agreed to raise bodies of infantry and cavalry to be called the Cinque Ports Volunteers. Both Harry and Will joined, as first and second lieutenants respectively. It was a fencible unit, one of many raised for defence against the threat of invasion during the French Revolutionary Wars. Harry was soon promoted captain and in 1799 attended a huge gathering of volunteers at Mote Park, near Maidstone, which was graced by the presence of George III and most of the royal family.[33] The French revolutionary threat later became the Napoleonic threat and as the unit remained operational until 1809, it is likely that the Mackeson brothers still had duties to perform. Will, at least, was still an active member in 1803.[34]

They were both also now family men. Harry had married Mary Jane Hayman on 14 September 1797 in Deal in a double ceremony with her brother William. Their father was well off and, on his death, left £2,000 to each of his children.[35] By 1813, Harry and Mary Jane were the parents of five daughters and a son. Will had married Harriet Reynolds just a week before his brother in the same church in Deal. They went on to have ten children. Fortunately, the brewery came with its own living accommodation, a spacious house called The Elms. Harry and his family lived there until at least 1881.[36]

But Harry, as well as being head of his own nuclear family, was now also head of the Mackeson clan. As well as Will, he had two other younger brothers, Jack and Thomas (Tom), and two sisters, Elizabeth and Mary. Then there were his half-siblings by his father's marriage to Clara Nickoll, Catherine (Kate) and Philip, not to mention a host of cousins on his mother's side. Many of these had been left legacies or annuities under John Friend's will and now considered that Harry Mackeson was responsible for administering their financial affairs. In fact, it was Will, not Harry, who had been named as John Friend's executor, but Will, it turned out, could not be relied upon to manage his own affairs, let alone anyone else's.

2

This Sweet Girl's Property

Jack was the next surviving sibling of Harry and Will Mackeson, baptised, like all his siblings, at Deal's St Leonard's church on 4 July 1777.

His early years are obscure, but by 1797 he was a commissioned lieutenant in the 7th Regiment of Native Infantry, part of the army of the East India Company (EIC).[1] He was the first of three Mackeson brothers to serve with the organisation. This dispersal of inconveniently large families to the colonies was becoming a feature of British life. America, since the War of Independence, was no longer welcoming; Australia was still a penal colony and Canada was largely unexplored by Europeans. This left India, though it was not strictly a colony as it was occupied and governed by the EIC.

Established in 1600 as a joint stock company, the EIC's founding charter gave it a monopoly of all trade between the Cape of Good Hope and the Strait of Magellan and authorised it to wage war to gain its ends. It was hugely successful and before long its reach was global, selling opium to China and tea to America, and controlling almost half the world's trade. The wording of the original charter was vague enough to allow the EIC to claim jurisdiction over all British subjects in Asia, raise fortifications, make laws, conduct an independent foreign policy, hold courts and imprison English subjects. It had its own army and a marine branch, the East Indiamen.

By the time Jack joined, it had become more or less respectable to serve with the EIC: its previous reputation as the employer of adventurers and fortune-seekers was diminishing. Rewards and promotions were good, and the EIC's army officers were among the best paid anywhere. There was the additional advantage for many like Jack that about 80 per cent of its officers were recruited from 'the middling sort', whereas the British Army's officer class was dominated by the scions of the landed gentry and the aristocracy, who could afford the cost of a commission. Promotion could also be quick: about one in four EIC soldiers died in India.[2] A contemporary author described junior officers in their leisure hours reading the almanacks:

> Making odd marks against each senior stager
> Of whose long sticking they were most jealous,
> As D for Death, and T for Turned out, his age or
> Infirmities, to see how soon they'd be a major.[3]

In 1802, Jack wrote to Harry from Kurria, a village in in Uttar Pradesh, wishing him well with the new brewery business and hoping that it 'will answer your expectations'.[4] He has, he says, been in action since December but this has been suspended during monsoon. ('In action' at that time and place generally meant subjugating the towns, cities and villages of the region to bring them under EIC jurisdiction.) It appears that he had entrusted management of his financial affairs to Harry and Will as he records his approval of their decisions on his behalf. He also says there is no prospect of him returning to England for the next sixteen years as, if he did, he would need £700 to £1,000 a year to live on.

He was promoted to captain in 1804 but the next year was back in England on furlough.[5] The EIC's rules were that after ten years' service, three years' home leave could be claimed, but Jack never returned to duty. Instead, he married 20-year-old Olive Mckeand in Walcot, Somerset, before setting out on a honeymoon trip that covered most of the spa towns in England – Cheltenham, Harrogate, Buxton, Matlock and Sheffield. Jack was frequently unwell, complaining of 'attacks of bile', including one on the night before his nuptials.[6] These could have been pain from gallstones, indigestion, migraines or something else. He does not describe his symptoms.

Olive was the Jamaica-born daughter of plantation owner Alexander Mckeand and his wife Elizabeth. As part of her marriage settlement, Olive received a coffee plantation on the island of her birth. Jack had been delighted to find out that his intended was a wealthy young woman. 'This sweet girl's property,' he wrote to Will in June 1805, 'is infinitely greater than my most sanguine imagination had an idea of. I understand that if her estates were converted into money that it will produce in this country at least £10,000 sterling.'[7] He is even more exultant than when he discovered he had inherited from John Friend.

The couple at first tried living in Hythe, where a son, William, was born in 1806. He lived only a few weeks. They then decided to travel to Jamaica to take control of the plantation, Blue Mountain. They arrived in March 1807 and at first stayed with Olive's relative, William Wyllis, at his sugar plantation, Mont Lebanus.[8] A daughter, Elizabeth, was born soon after their arrival and seven more children, including twins, followed.

The Jamaican coffee boom was short-lived and Jack got into it at the wrong time. The principal market was continental Europe (the British still preferred tea, which was cheaper) but Napoleon closed this in 1806 by implementing his Continental System, which excluded all British goods, including those from the colonies. A second thriving market, the USA, was hampered by the American Embargo Act of 1809 and the War of 1812 between Britain and America.

Jack wrote to Harry and his stepmother, Clara, once a year or so. His great expectations, first of his inheritance from John Friend and then of his wife's wealth, had been dashed and he lived in permanent anticipation of financial disaster. This was always the fault of someone, or something, else. In 1811 he wrote, 'Unless some change takes place, we will sink altogether.' In 1812 it was, 'This country is in a deplorable state and a vast number of people are completely ruined.' There had been a violent storm and 'a most dreadful earthquake which almost shook the house to the ground'. In 1813 he wrote that 'funds are very low indeed' and that the coffee he had in store had rotted. The slave trade had been abolished in 1807, so there was no longer a supply of new labour and Jack blamed this for his situation. 'You ask why the planters do not send more sugar home. The abolition of the slave trade is the principal cause. Great numbers of Estates are obliged to be thrown up for want of strength to work them.'[9]

Owning slaves in the Colonies was still, however, legal and Jack had around 120. He now started to grumble about the cost of them. In 1813 he wrote to Clara, 'I wish to add ten or twenty negroes to my strength, which would set me back some £2,000.' He went on:

> I am sensible the Negroes in this island are above the common class of people at home in points of living and domestic comforts. The industrious Negro has a good and comfortable house, plenty of pigs and fowl, & bread in abundance. They are supplied regularly with salt fish by their owners and they have gardens. They are, I think, comparatively speaking, much happier than the labourer at home.[10]

These words parrot the public pronouncements of the Caribbean authorities when challenged as to the morality of slave ownership. John Brathwaite, another plantation and slave owner and agent for the island of Barbados, travelled to London in 1788 to give testimony to the British government's inquiry into slavery:

> It was not uncommon, he said, for slaves to suffer for food when corn [bread stuff] was high or a sugar crop failed. Industrious Negroes, of course, raised some provisions, hogs, and poultry about their own huts or on allotments. Even so, he thought a slave was as well off as a free Negro and better than an English labourer with a family.[11]

Jack's financial situation did not improve and in 1814 he had debts amounting to £5,000. He then decided that this was the fault of Harry and Will. He had been too young, he wrote, when their father died, to understand what they intended to do with his money.[12]

He and his family returned to England in 1817 and went first to stay in Hythe before moving to Bath to a house in Widcombe Crescent, only twenty minutes' walk from the fashionable Pump Room, built above the old Roman Baths. Jane Austen, who lived in Bath, wrote that everyone 'was to be seen in the room at different periods of the fashionable hours; crowds of people were every moment passing in and out'.[13]

Jack was still pleading poverty, which he now laid at the door of his 'over-liberal' agents in Jamaica. He owed £2,000 and had outgoings of £1,300 a year. He complained that he could not afford to have the house he had just taken for three years 'new painted and papered'.[14] Will regularly sent him money, even though his own finances were in a parlous state.

Broke or not, the *Bath Chronicle* recorded that Jack and Olive continued to attend fashionable events in Bath. For a while Jack considered returning to India, but was persuaded by his in-laws that the heat there would be injurious to Olive, who was 'naturally of a very bilious habit'.[15]

On 16 April 1828 Clara Mackeson wrote to her stepson Harry that, 'Jack has left Bath & has a large house within 7 miles & Mrs Mackeson has charge of his 6 children from the West Indies. I think she has her hands full adding her own 6 to the number.'[16] Of Jack and Olive's eight children, Elizabeth had married and Isabella had died at the age of 2, which accounts for the reference to Olive's six children. The allusion to 'his children from the West Indies' presumably means that Jack brought over his illegitimate children, probably from a liaison with an enslaved or free woman of colour. There are no records to show these children's names, either in Jamaica or the UK, so these additions to the Mackeson family must for the present remain anonymous and their fortunes unknown.

The move was to Bradford Leigh House, near Trowbridge, but the stay was short. Two years later, Jack sold all the house's furnishings, including china, glass, books and 'a fine toned six-octave Piano Forte'.[17] It seems he moved to France, probably to Normandy. The eldest unmarried daughter, Olive Ann, was married in Paris in December

1830 and her brother John, the eldest son, died 'near Caen' in 1834.[18] Some years later, Jack's son, William Wyllis Mackeson, described his father as being 'of Blue Mountain, Jamaica, and of Caen, Normandy'.[19] Why he left the country remains a mystery, although given his history, it is likely that money troubles played a part in his decision.

In 1835, however, Jack received a windfall. When slaver ownership in the colonies was finally abolished the previous year, the British government promised 'compensation' to all slave owners. For the 132 slaves Jack had owned, he received £2,446 9*s* 8*d*.[20]

Some of Jack's children returned to the West Indies. Olive Ann, widowed young, died in Spanish Town in 1840; William Wyllis Mackeson, the fifth child, practised law in Jamaica and was a member of the Assembly. Jack himself revisited at least once and died on the return journey on board the *Tulloch Castle* in 1843.[21] Neither his will nor probate have been found. Olive went to live in Jersey with her unmarried daughters.

3

A Most Amiable and Unaffected Young Woman

The fourth Mackeson brother was Tom, born on 16 January 1780 in Deal,[1] the sixth child of Henry Mackeson and his second wife. He replaced an earlier son called Thomas, who had lived only a few months. At the age of 13, like his elder brother Jack, he joined the EIC, but in the maritime service as a seaman, rather than in the Company's army.[2] The EIC, in common with the regular British forces, expected its officers to provide their own uniform and other necessities. As he was still a minor when he joined up, the executors of his father's will gave him an advance of £850 to provide for this.[3]

His first ship, the *Taunton Castle*, took him to China. There followed more ships, more voyages to the Far East and regular promotions: he was fifth mate aboard the *Lord Hawkesbury*; fourth and third mate on the *Carnatic 2*; second mate on the *Europe* and finally captain of the *Sarah Christiana* in 1804.[4]

On 6 July 1805 he was granted a letter of marque.[5] A letter of marque and reprisal was a government licence that authorised a private person, a 'privateer', to attack and capture vessels of a nation at war with the issuer. Once captured, the privateers could bring the case of that prize before their own admiralty court for transfer of ownership to themselves. John's father, Henry, had also benefitted in this way in his seagoing days.

The reason for this letter of marque was that the *Sarah Christiana* was about to take part, with other East Indiamen, in the expedition under General Sir David Baird and Admiral Sir Home Riggs Popham to capture the Dutch Cape Colony. Tom's ship carried supplies and troops, sailing from Cork in September 1806 and reaching the Cape in January the next year. The Dutch governor capitulated the same month.

Tom sailed on to Madras and Calcutta and then homewards via St Helena, reaching Falmouth on April 1807. Two further trips to India followed, though the second was nearly his last. In December 1809, in Calcutta, he was attacked by one of his own crew with a hatchet. He was visiting the sick quarters at the time with the ship's surgeon, who was able to assist him.[6] The would-be assassin was charged with mutiny and sentenced to death in March 1810 but by then Tom was on his way back to England.[7]

At some point in all this travelling, he had managed to meet Mary Selby, fall in love and propose marriage. The wedding took place on 11 April 1812. She was the eldest daughter of Thomas Selby of Otford Castle near Sevenoaks. Despite its grand name, her family home was the remains of a Tudor episcopal palace to which was annexed a more modern edifice. A few weeks after their marriage, the couple met Tom's brother-in-law, Peter Fisher, who reported back to Harry Mackeson in Hythe, 'Mrs Mackeson really appears a most amiable and unaffected young woman and I have no doubt will tend to secure his happiness in this life'.[8]

Tom and Mary produced three children: Lumsden in 1815 (named for Thomas's friend Colonel Thomas Lumsden); Edward in 1817; and Mary Louisa in 1830. Lumsden was apparently a 'disappointing child', but grew up to be a respectable lawyer.[9] All the children married, but none presented Tom and Mary with a grandchild.

Tom took his EIC pension in 1836 and retired to Hythe, where he lived in St Leonard's House (otherwise known as the Old Manor House), former home of the Deedes family. With him were his wife and daughter and a niece, Mary Parkinson, his late sister Elizabeth's child. He stood successfully for election to the Town Council together with his brother Harry and became an alderman.

Tom and Mary later moved to Walmer, between Dover and Deal, and then to Weston, near Bath, where Tom died on 2 November 1854.

4

So Iniquitous, So Disgraceful, a Business

Henry Mackeson had two daughters with his second wife, Elizabeth Bean: Elizabeth and Mary. We know only the bare bones of Elizabeth's life. She was baptised at St Leonard's church in Deal on 20 January 1779 and married Thomas Parkinson on 17 September 1798 at the same church. He was a dentist 'of Radlett Court, Fleet Street'.[1] They had eight children and lived in Brook Street, off Bond Street in London, though Elizabeth's burial record gives her residence as Hythe. Elizabeth died on 9 October 1823 and is buried in the Mackeson vault at St Leonard's church. A fading stone obscurely placed on the parapet above the vault is her only memorial.

Thomas Parkinson died in 1836. It seems he did not have a lot to leave his children, as Peter Fisher wrote the next year that, 'The poor Parkinsons are left in very confined and scant circumstances'.[2]

Of Mary, the youngest child of Henry Mackeson and Elizabeth Bean, we know a great deal more. She was baptised in St Leonard's church, Deal, on 26 June 1782. Her mother died the next year. She married Peter Fisher, a captain in the Royal Navy, on 24 June 1803 at St Mary Magdalene church, Woolwich. Her husband was either already a great friend of Mary's brother, Harry, or became one. The two wrote to each other frequently and Harry, in his meticulous way, kept nearly all the letters.

Close friends they may have been, but they observed the etiquette of the day and only ever used each other's surnames. Peter's letters were addressed to 'My Dear Mackeson' and he always referred to Harry's wife as Mrs Mackeson.

Peter was the son of the Rev. Peter Fisher, Rector of Little Torrington in Devon. His family was not, however, as respectable as this might suggest. In the first place, the Rev. Fisher had, scandalously, fathered an illegitimate child on a parishioner during the 1770s. Then one of Peter's sisters, Sarah, took advantage of the absence of parental control when her father died in 1803 and immediately went on the stage. In the early nineteenth century, being an actress was scarcely respectable. Sarah then married another actor and moved to London where, as Mrs Egerton, she regularly appeared at Covent Garden until the 1830s. She is never mentioned in Peter's correspondence.

After their marriage, Mary and Peter Fisher went to live in Barnstaple, where the first of their eleven children, Owen, was born. The other babies followed at regular intervals and for a time Mary's stepmother, Clara, and her half-sister Kate moved in with the family.[3] Mary must have dreaded getting pregnant. She suffered a great deal and after Owen's birth was 'very weak and cannot eat'. With the next pregnancy, Peter wrote that, 'Mary is unwell & only moves from her bedroom to go & lie on the couch all day', and he noted during later pregnancies that she suffered from pains in her legs. Of her labours he commented, 'She suffers the most excruciating torment.'[4]

They stayed in Devon for some years, but were back in Kent by 1813. Three children were born in Hythe and the last three in Walmer.

One or more of the Fisher children or Mary was almost always ill and Peter, when at home, took a great interest in their treatment. Leeches were much favoured. They were applied to Mary's painful legs when she was pregnant and to her head when she was 'overwhelmed' by news that her son William was to be sent abroad with the army. They were used to treat the children's fevers and chickenpox. Sometimes, other remedies were tried. After Mary's final confinement, Peter ordered from Hythe a 6-gallon cask of Mackeson mild ale to help her recovery.[5]

By way of preventative medicine, he advised Harry Mackeson that his own daughter had very much wanted to go out in society with its temptations 'but by resisting these and keeping quietly at home, she has kept her health'. Harry had reported one of his daughters was ill, which Peter blamed on attending too many balls.

The other children, however, gave Peter and Mary plenty to worry about. The eldest, Owen, died aged 22 and the fifth, John, aged only 14. Thomas, the second son, joined the Royal Navy but in 1839, as a lieutenant, was found guilty of drunkenness while on duty on Christmas Eve. He rallied and eventually became an admiral. The next son, Peter, also joined the Royal Navy but in 1836 disappeared, having obtained a discharge from his ship and writing that he intended to live under an assumed name. The escapade did not last long: his father found him another ship and he covered himself in glory in action off Spain.

His younger brother, William, was a particular trial to his parents and to Harry Mackeson. He chose the army as a career, but could not resist the temptations of the mess. He ran up enormous bills, which he could not pay and his father was obliged to save his honour by giving him £1,500. Of this, £1,000 was an advance on his eventual legacy and £500 a loan, but William did not repay this or settle his debts. When his father died in 1844, William made it clear that he expected to receive his legacy in full. His brothers were horrified and refused to countenance 'so iniquitous, so disgraceful, a business', accusing him of taking advantage of his widowed mother and fatherless sisters and even of being 'a primary cause of his father's death'. The executor of Peter Fisher's will, Harry Mackeson, agreed and refused to rescue William from 'the lamentable consequences of his extravagance'.[6]

The youngest son, Edward, had a smoother army career after a disappointing academic record at the Military Academy in Woolwich and went on to become a general.

Of the girls, Mary, the Fishers' eldest daughter, seems to have suffered the fate of many eldest daughters. With her father frequently away at sea, she became her mother's carer and when Mary senior decamped to Boulogne for a couple of years in the late 1820s (Peter believed the

French sea air would be better for her: it actually made no difference), Mary junior went too, under orders not to leave her alone. After her father's death, Mary stayed with her mother, looking after her and the family finances. Later she lived with a maiden Fisher aunt, still in Walmer, and died there in 1875.

Susanna, the second daughter, was in constant ill health throughout her life but lived to be 75; Elizabeth married a solicitor, Martin Daniel, who later did a lot of work for the Mackesons in their complicated family affairs; Harriet had a short-lived engagement to a member of the Leith family, who owned vast swathes of land in Walmer and Deal. Her father was relieved when she broke it off: 'He was not the person in whose keeping I could place my daughter's happiness.'[7] She later married an Irish army officer.

Peter died in 1844 and Mary in 1861. Both are buried in St Mary's church, Walmer.

5

THIS UNFORTUNATE CIRCUMSTANCE

Catherine Mackeson, always Kate to her family, was the only daughter of Henry Mackeson and his third wife, Clara Nickoll, and was baptised in Deal on 25 January 1785. At the age of 17, she married Thomas May and they moved to Thomas's home village of Littlebourne, not far from Canterbury. Two sons were born before Thomas's untimely death in 1805. Catherine, at 20, was a widow with two babies and although her husband had been possessed of a large house, it seems that either he had little ready money or possibly large debts. Whichever was the case, the marital home, Littlebourne Court, was sold. The sale was handled by Thomas's brother, John May, an attorney. He advertised it as a dwelling house with three cottages, two barns, greenhouses with grape vines and 260 acres of land.[1]

Kate went to live with her mother, who now had a house in Lambeth, and it was there that she married again, to Edward Kingsford, in 1814. Her new husband, though from a prosperous family of east Kent millers, did not meet with family approval. Three years earlier, Harry Mackeson had discovered that Kate had lent Kingsford £400 to help start up a 'silk manufactory'. He demanded that Kingsford provide security.[2] In Hythe, Mrs Wildash, the local doctor's wife, wrote to Harry about 'the intended connection between your sister and Mr Kingsford'. She asked Harry for an interview as she said she had information about him.[3] This was unlikely to have been complimentary. Kate had also upset her brother-in-law, John May, by writing to the Secretary to the Treasury recommending Edward Kingsford for a post and naming John as a sponsor. In fact, he was no such thing. John wrote angrily to Kate that while Mr Kingsford 'may be a very deserving young man', he was 'exceedingly indignant at the liberty you have taken of using my name'.[4]

John May was so angry about his sister-in-law's marriage that he cut off his connection with her. He had previously supported her financially and had agreed to pay for his nephews' education, but now withdrew this offer. Edward Kingsford wrote to Harry in Hythe asking for money, explaining that he was in no position to support his new stepsons as he and Kate had a joint income of less than £200 per annum.[5] It was not an auspicious start to their married life.

They settled in Lambeth and somehow Edward bought a mill and got a contract with the Royal Navy Victualling Office. It may be that this was in part financed by Harry Mackeson, as Kingsford asked him for a loan of a £1,000 in 1821, though he had no security to offer beyond a life insurance policy.[6]

He was not a very successful miller. In 1824 alone, three consignments of his biscuit meal were rejected by the Navy as being unfit for purpose.[7] Then, in December 1829, he was declared bankrupt. His mother-in-law, Clara Mackeson, wrote to Harry in Hythe to tell him. This was, she said, a disaster for everyone. She would have to give up her house in Lambeth as she had invested all her money in Kingsford's business.[8]

Kate and Edward, who now had two children together, moved back to east Kent and set up a school – Wickham House Preparatory School near Littlebourne, where 'young Gentlemen are boarded and instructed in the Latin, French, German & English languages and every other branch of knowledge'.[9] Two years later they moved to new premises in St Martin's Hill, Canterbury, and established the Stone House Classical Academy, which offered fencing and gymnastics as well as academic subjects.[10]

This school, too, was short-lived. In 1835, Catherine swallowed her pride and wrote to Harry, from whom she had become estranged:

> It is a length of years since I have had the pleasure of addressing you and however much I may have regretted this unfortunate circumstance, believe me it has been quite unsought for on my part. It is therefore doubly painful to my feelings to be obliged to do it for pecuniary affairs.[11]

In short, she and Edward were about to be evicted.

It seems that Harry relented and gave them more money, as the next we hear they have established a 'Classical and Commercial school' in the Vicarage House, Patrixbourne, only a couple of miles from Littlebourne.[12] It was, Kate wrote, 'well adapted for a school. All our pupils have followed us and we have added two more. Mother is much better.' Her mother Clara, now penniless, lived with the couple throughout their vicissitudes.[13]

Kate herself was not quite penniless. She still had £1,339 from the will of her father, which her husband could not touch. The legacy was administered by Harry and his brother Tom and by her son Thomas May, now a barrister. It was sensibly invested in 3 per cent Consols, producing an income of £40 a year.[14]

This was not enough to live on and when the school failed, as inevitably it did, Kate and Edward moved in with their married daughter, Elizabeth Broad, and her husband in Kensington. Kate died of asthma and bronchitis on 16 November 1854 and is buried in Kensal Green cemetery. Edward died in 1866.

6

A Very Fine Young Man

Philip was the last child of Henry Mackeson, born to his wife Clara Nickoll on 5 August 1788. At the age of 11 he entered the King's School in Canterbury as a King's Scholar, which entitled him to free tuition. These scholarships were awarded after a boy had been interviewed by the Dean and some of the Chapter of Canterbury Cathedral, and were, theoretically at least, based on academic ability. By the time of Philip's admission, however, the school was at a low ebb and another successful candidate commented that intake was so low 'that the Dean and Chapter were, I suppose, more anxious to give admission than to refuse it to anyone'.[1]

Philip left the King's School at Christmas 1802 to attend Mr Henderson's school in Streatham, where he learnt, in addition to the three Rs, Latin, dancing and geography.[2] His father was now dead and his school fees were paid by his elder half-brother, Harry Mackeson, who also footed the bill for Philip's school clothes.[3]

When he was 14, an apprenticeship was arranged for him, by Harry, at the offices of Robert de Lasaux, an attorney of Ashford, Kent. De Lasaux wrote to Harry that he would 'be happy to take a young person of such respectable Connections as your brother into my office as an Articled Clerk'.[4] The premium, also paid by Harry, was £305 and it was arranged that Philip would live with the de Lasaux family. He was duly fitted out, again at Harry's expense, with a wardrobe suitable for his new position: black silk breeches, a black silk tabby

The King's School, Canterbury in 1777. *The King's School*

(plain weave) waistcoat, a Brighton jacket lined with calico and a black cloth lapelled coat 'with extra pocket', all supplied by J. Read, Draper and Tailor of Deal.[5]

The position only lasted a couple of years. Philip's half-brother Jack had recently returned home from India. Perhaps inspired by his stories of derring-do, Philip applied on 26 April 1805 to the EIC for a place as a cadet in their military service.[6] He was accepted and Harry, having presumably lost the premium he paid to de Lasaux, now parted with £105 to kit his half-brother out.[7]

This could be an expensive business. One guide to newcomers to India recommended that a man should take four dozen each of calico shirts and undershirts; six dozen pairs of stockings of various lengths and fabrics; four dozen neckerchiefs and the same quantity of handkerchiefs, as well as bedding (including a mattress) and cutlery.[8]

Philip sailed to Bombay on board the SS *Sir William Poultney* in July 1805.[9] The Bombay archipelago had the best natural harbour in South Asia and had early in the history of the EIC become its premier naval base. The next year found him with the 1st Native Infantry. In 1807 he was promoted to ensign and then in 1811 to lieutenant.[10] A friend of his brother-in-law Peter Fisher met him at about this time and reported that he had 'become a very fine young man'.[11]

This fine young man, though, had a secret life.

Philip made his will in October 1817 at Mutah, in the wet district of Meghalaya in north-eastern India. He left everything to 'my child Philip Mackeson, begotten from a native Girl'. He asked that after his own death, his son be sent to England together with his sword and any of his clothes that may be useful, and left his 'girl', Secunna, 300 rupees in recognition of 'her excellent conduct'. He asked his friends, Lieutenants Lister and Hake, to take care of matters in India and his mother to look after his child. In the event of Clara's death, young Philip was entrusted to the care of Harry and Will Mackeson. An undated codicil, written 'on the banks of the river Khyber', stated that he feared Secunna was pregnant again and that he wanted his property divided between the two children. His mistress, or *bibi*, would now receive 600 rupees and he regretted that he could not do more to support her.[12]

Philip, by then a brevet captain, died of 'spasmodic cholera' on 9 March 1819 in camp near Asseeghut.[13] An epidemic of the disease (sometimes called Asiatic cholera or cholera morbus) had started in Bengal in 1816 and had spread throughout the sub-continent. It went on to become a global pandemic. Cholera led to a horrible death. Nausea and dizziness were succeeded by violent vomiting and diarrhoea; extreme muscular cramps followed by an insatiable thirst before the final, 'sinking stage' when the pulse dropped and lethargy set in. Its cause was then unknown. Many treatments were tried but none worked and there were no vaccines until the late nineteenth century.

The Mackeson family must have known that the mortality rate among EIC soldiers was high, but the news would still have been a shock, considerably compounded by the revelation that they were now responsible for two small children who lived 4,000 miles away and of whose existence they had probably been completely unaware.

It is unlikely that Philip shared the details of his family life in his letters home. He had been in India for fourteen years by the time of his death and mores were different there. Many officers had *bibis*, and, often, children with them. It was not considered particularly scandalous. The arrangements were generally ignored by the EIC hierarchy but in 1786, Lord Cornwallis, the Governor General, had issued an order banning the Anglo-Indian orphans of British soldiers from travelling to England to be educated.[14] Little Philip Mackeson was not destined to meet his English family.

He was 9 or 10 years old when his father died. Secunna had also given birth to a baby girl, named Clara for her English grandmother. She was probably only a year old. Lt Lister did his best by them, but it was not easy as Philip, far from having enough money to support his children, had died in debt, with an unpaid mess bill. Maintaining a *bibi* was an expensive undertaking: Secunna would have expected her own establishment together with servants and enough funds to keep them all. The cost of such an arrangement was estimated to be about £60 a year.[15] Philip's lack of provision for his family was not an unusual situation. One contemporary French commentator remarked 'how few British fathers can leave anything to their Anglo-Indian children at their deaths'.[16] Philip did, however, leave property in England, which passed to his mother in order, he had hoped, that she could raise his children.

By 1825, Philip junior had been placed in a 'charitable institution', in Bombay, probably the Orphan Institution, supported by the EIC through compulsory deductions from the pay of its officers. It had been founded in 1782 for the children of deceased officers 'legitimate or otherwise'.[17] Both children were baptised in 1826. Philip's mother Clara desperately wanted them to come to her in England, even though this was impossible, and as a result refused to pass her guardianship of them, and the means of support, to Lt Lister. Harry was concerned about the children, too, particularly as he did not trust his stepmother's grasp of financial matters. In 1828, he received a visit from his brother-in-law Peter Fisher, whose friend had seen Lister and the children in Bombay and told him that the children were in a 'dreadful situation'. Harry wrote to Clara telling her to make her will and not to risk in any way Philip's English property, which would pass to the children.[18]

She failed to take his advice and lost all her own money and Philip's when her son-in-law Edward Kingsford was declared bankrupt. Lister, now a major, and his wife took the children in. Philip junior worked for Lister as a clerk and little Clara was 'made useful'. It was all they could do, as they had only Lister's army pay to live on and had half-a-dozen children of their own.[19]

There is no direct evidence that Harry contributed to the upkeep of the children after Clara lost her money. He was under no obligation to do so, but, as ever, absence of evidence is not evidence of absence. Major Lister, on home leave, visited Harry in Hythe in September 1834.[20] What transpired between them is unknown, but it is possible that funds were made available to Lister or the children.

As an adult, Philip junior went into business with John Montagu Farnworth and Merwanjee Cooverjee in Bombay, importing and selling luxury European foodstuffs, alcohol and perfumery from their 'godown' or warehouse in Meadow Street. This was a popular area with the British, in an area known as 'Ingrez Bazaar' because of the number of English shops in the vicinity. Farnworth left the concern in 1837, as did Philip the following year.[21] He found employment as a deputy collector of taxes at Jalandhar in the Punjab and died there on 4 November 1849 aged 40. His death notice in the *Bombay Times and Journal of Commerce* refers to him as 'P. Mackeson, Esq.' He had become respectable. It is not known if he married or had children.

Philip's younger sister, Clara, married, in Bombay on 1 March 1834, Henry Tudor, a 'Free Mariner' and captain of the ship *Sir Charles Malcolm*.[22] He was licensed by the EIC to trade to the east of the Cape of Good Hope and in some years to travel to England as an 'extra' East Indiaman. It was a very short-lived marriage, as Henry died, aged 32, five months later.[23]

Philip Mackeson's autograph, carefully carved into his desk. *The King's School*

The union did, however, have an outcome. On 29 January 1835, Clara 'the lady of the late Captain H. Tudor' gave birth to a son.[24] Clara Mackeson, the illegitimate daughter of a penurious Englishman and an Indian *bibi*, was also now respectable. Little Henry Tudor, named for his father, was baptised in May that year.[25] Sadly, he died aged 16 months.[26] Clara was still alive, though where is unknown, in 1837, when she inherited some jewellery from her late husband's brother, Richard.[27] Of Secunna, the children's mother, there is no further trace.

Philip's children may be lost to us, but he did leave tangible evidence of his existence. As a pupil at the King's School, like so many schoolboys before and since, he carved his name into the hard oak of the pews and desks reserved in Canterbury Cathedral for the school. When the old seats were removed in 1879 to make room for new choir stalls, some of these were preserved, including that occupied by P. Mackeson.

7

HYTHE IS HALF BARRACKS

While their siblings had adventures and misadventures, Harry and Will Mackeson were getting on with the business of running a brewery and raising their own numerous families.

Brewing in the early nineteenth century was a blend of skill, science and agriculture. Transforming water, barley, hops and yeast into good beer required both meticulous cookery and heavy labour.

First, the barley had to be malted. It was screened to remove grit and then steeped in water in massive cisterns for up to three days before being drained down, allowing germination to begin. The damp grains were then spread on a malting floor and turned occasionally to prevent the grain roots from knotting themselves together. After a week or two, the part-germinated grains were dried in a kiln to stop the growth and add flavour and colour. The process up to this point took place in a floor maltings, which needed a large, well-ventilated floor area. Typically, these buildings were long and low with regular windows. The malthouse at Hythe, part of which is still standing, is typical, though it has now lost the square kiln that once abutted the High Street.

The malt was then milled. At the Mackesons' brewery this was done with rotatable millstones, though mechanical steam rollers were by then available. It was then mixed in a mash tun with mineralised water known as liquor. The sweet liquid that was run off from under the mash tun was now known as wort and was boiled with hops in a copper.

The Mackesons' malthouse, now used as an antiques market. *Author's collection*

The hopped wort was sieved and cooled, then put into fermenting vessels and yeast added. The froth was skimmed off. Fermentation would take about five days. The resultant beer was then matured in oak casks, before being bottled. The wort from the mash tun could be used again to produce successively weaker beers in a process called parti-gyling.

The Mackesons also produced porter, so called because it had become a popular drink with London's porters. It was made by combining strong and weak worts and was highly hopped. Its dark colour was achieved by using dark malt or, later, adding burnt sugar. It needed to be matured for some time in butts (casks holding 109 gallons) before sale.

By 1801, England was mid-Industrial Revolution, transforming the way people worked. Brewing was an industry and brewers were industrialists. They were as affected by the developments of the time as any other manufacturer; indeed, the brewing industry was an important pioneer of some technological advances. The Mackesons could now take advantage of hydrometers, thermometers and steam engines. The first patent for a mashing machine had been filed in 1787. These inventions laid the technical basis for the mechanical and scientific rationalisation of the industry through the nineteenth century and no brewer who wished to remain competitive could afford to ignore them.

Hydrometers were used to measure the density of a liquid and had been around since the time of Archimedes, but in the late eighteenth century an officer in the employ of HM Excise, Bartholomew Sikes, devised a system of 'alcoholometry'. He designed a metal hydrometer and compiled tables for use in conjunction with it, which, together, provided a simple means of determining the strength of alcoholic beverages. All that had to be done was to float the hydrometer in the liquid, observe the hydrometer reading, take the temperature of the sample and then consult the tables. While this was useful for brewers, it was of even more value to HM Excise for revenue purposes and in 1818 its use became compulsory.

Harry and Will employed the services of a master brewer to manage the production process. In these early days, he was John Levesque, a member of a London brewing family descended from Huguenot immigrants. He was in Hythe from at least 1805, when his first child was baptised in St Leonard's church in the town. Five more children followed until 1814 and it seems likely that the family then returned to London. John's wife died there in 1824 and John took over his father's brewery in Old Street. He was the author of two books on brewing, including in 1836, *The Art of Brewing and Fermenting in the Summer.*

Cleanliness in the brewery was vital. The casks had to be scalded and then left to dry completely. Every utensil had to be washed and scrubbed with birch brooms. All the vessels except the coppers were made of wood. The mash tuns needed to hold both heat and water and wood was a good insulator. A reliable supply of clean, good-quality water was essential both for hygiene and for brewing good beer. The moderately hard water of Hythe, filtered through the chalk of the North Downs, was ideal for the pale ales that became popular in the nineteenth century.

Since at least the seventeenth century, Hythe's water had been supplied from springs that fed a cistern located uphill of the town in a field known as the Dentalls. The water was delivered to three conduits along the High Street, at the east and west ends and in the middle at the 'Great Conduit' (remembered today by Great Conduit Street). These arrangements met the needs of the small town, until the soldiers arrived in numbers. In 1804 Harry and Will attended a meeting of Hythe corporation. They reported that they were 'very distressed for water in consequence of the demand for it by the number of Military who have come'.[1] However, the brothers had not come to beg. Apparently at their own expense they had conveyed extra spring water to the Great Conduit, but the pipes could not cope with the additional supplies. They offered to pay for more piping of at least 2in diameter and this would mean more water for the town. As the cost would be at least £170, the assembly agreed. Regrettably, the unintended consequence was that the increase in water pressure caused many of Hythe's old, smaller-gauge, pipes to burst and they had to be replaced, at a cost to the corporation of £20.[2]

Hops, barley and other necessities such as horse hay and oats had to be brought in from outside the town. Production of barley in Kent was in decline from the early nineteenth century and sometimes the Mackesons bought it in from further afield. They traded with dealers in Ipswich, from whence the barley was carried by ship. The voyage to Dover took ten days and insurance rates could be high. When ships were endangered by the enemy – the French – in the Channel or on the North Sea insurance rates rose. In 1803 Harry insured 482 quarters of Ipswich malt for £1,450.[3] A quarter was the standard measure for barley as bought by the maltster and weighed about 448lb, which yielded about 80 to 100lb for the brewer.

Hops, used for flavour and as a preservative, could be obtained nearer home, as the crop had been widely grown in Kent since the sixteenth century. One contemporary brewer believed that the best hops were grown very near Hythe, 'No hop in my opinion can equal a fine East Kent, for its flavour, condition and good quality for keeping beer.'[4]

A 'keeping beer' was one that could be stored for nine to twelve months. The Mackesons agreed with him and usually bought their hops from Bridge, near Canterbury, but sometimes had to look further afield.

Local carriers were used for short trips. In 1812 one submitted his account for bringing barley from Folkestone and Dover (where it had been landed), for delivering 'cols' to the 'brouse' and carrying 'bear' in 'barels'. He also charged for 'goan to Dover for Hops'.[5] One can almost hear his Kentish accent. For deliveries to or via London, the Mackesons used the local hoy, weather permitting. If the sea was rough, goods were delivered to Dover, which had a proper harbour, but this involved the extra cost of temporary storage.[6]

However, as well as costs, there were opportunities. These were presented inadvertently by Napoleon, who was threatening to invade England. The threat was real. In 1803 there were at least 100,000 soldiers encamped at Boulogne with over 2,000 barges waiting for the

One of the two remaining Martello Towers in Hythe. *Oast House Archive, CC BY-SA-20*

order to sail. Spies reconnoitred the coast between Folkestone and Rye for suitable landing places. The English (after rejecting the idea of flooding the Romney Marsh) responded with coastal defences and from 1805 to 1808, twenty-seven Martello towers were built along the Kent coast, from No. 1 to the north of Folkestone to No. 27 in St Mary's Bay. Ten metres high, each tower incorporated half a million bricks laid with hot lime and its construction used a great deal of manpower.

At the same time, another defensive work was under construction: the Royal Military Canal. Started in 1804, it ran 28 miles from Seabrook to Hastings via Hythe and was dug by the army using 1,000 soldiers from all over the country. In Hythe, the War Office seized land, including some belonging to the Mackesons, without any very clear indication of how they might be reimbursed. William Deedes (kinsman of the William Deedes who built Sandling Park) was now one of the town's MPs and organised a committee to make representations to the government. Harry was one of those deputed to scrutinise any offers made.[7] It was his first foray into public life and would not be repeated for some years.

The Royal Military Canal at Hythe, now the domain of ducks and gulls.
Author's collection

It has been estimated that between 1801 and 1811, the resident population of Hythe rose to more than 2,000, quite apart from the soldiers and labourers working on building the Martello Towers and digging the canal.[8] There were barracks in Saltwood and a developing military encampment at nearby Shorncliffe. These were all thirsty men and the Mackeson brothers were happy to satisfy their needs. Sergeants regularly bought a 'barel of beer', perhaps for their mess or to refresh the men who spent their days labouring.[9]

Officers, too, needed refreshment. For their entertainment and that of their ladies, balls were held at the town hall and a theatre opened in 1804 (remembered now in Theatre Street). Both venues would have served wine and beer.

As they paid the outstanding instalments on the brewery, Harry and Will acquired several inns. In Hythe they added the Duke's Head, the King's Head and the Swan to the Red Lion and the White Hart. There were also another dozen inns at villages and small towns on the Romney Marsh and in Ashford. They would add to these as time went on.

The Swan in Hythe was a particularly useful acquisition. It was used as an auction house so provided a captive clientele on sale days. It was also a coaching inn and travelling, too, is a thirsty business. The White Hart, only yards away along Hythe High Street, was also a Post and Excise House and hired post-chaises 'to anywhere in England'.[10] It was adjacent to the town hall and there was a useful door at first-floor level between the two buildings, giving the members of the corporation access to a robing room and, of course, to refreshments after a long meeting.

The Marsh inns served more or less as community centres for the small populations of the towns and villages, which lacked any other convenient meeting place. Inquests were held in them, tithes were collected, wages paid and smugglers hatched their plots there. All these activities also required sustenance. The brothers continued to acquire public houses and trade was good. By 1821 they owned twenty inns and the whole business was valued at nearly £44,000.[11]

The Swan Hotel in Hythe High Street. *Author's collection*

The White Hart and the town hall. *Author's collection*

In 1815 joyful news had arrived of Wellington's victory at Waterloo. Although the Napoleonic threat was over, the military did not immediately desert Hythe. The Royal Staff Corps had built substantial barracks in 1810 to accommodate over 300 men and the bulk of the personnel of the Royal Waggon Train had moved there, too. 'Hythe is half barracks,' William Cobbett wrote. Although he disapproved, it would have been good news for local traders.[12] The future for the Mackesons must have seemed reasonably secure.

And then Will died.

THE FAMILY OF HENRY ('HARRY') MACKESON

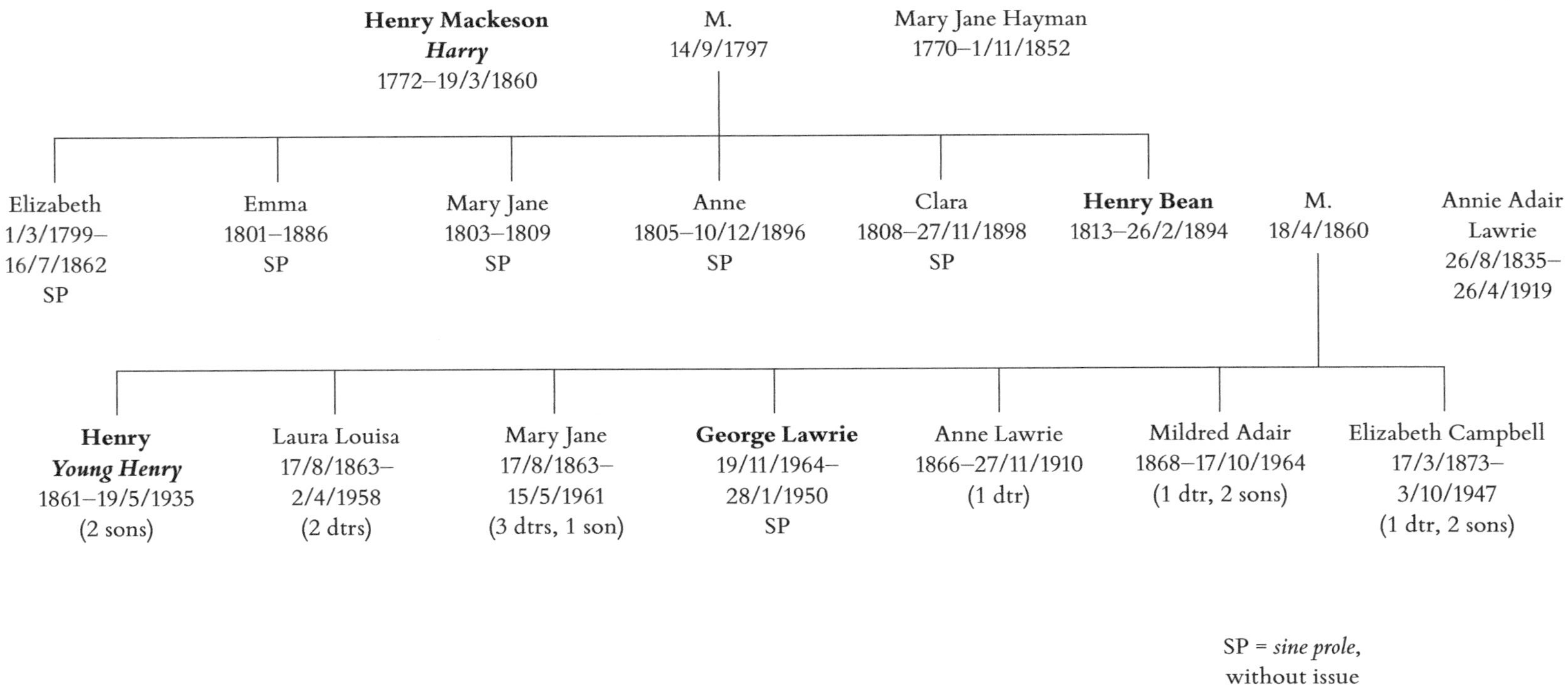

The descendants of Harry Mackeson.

The Family of William ('Will') Mackeson

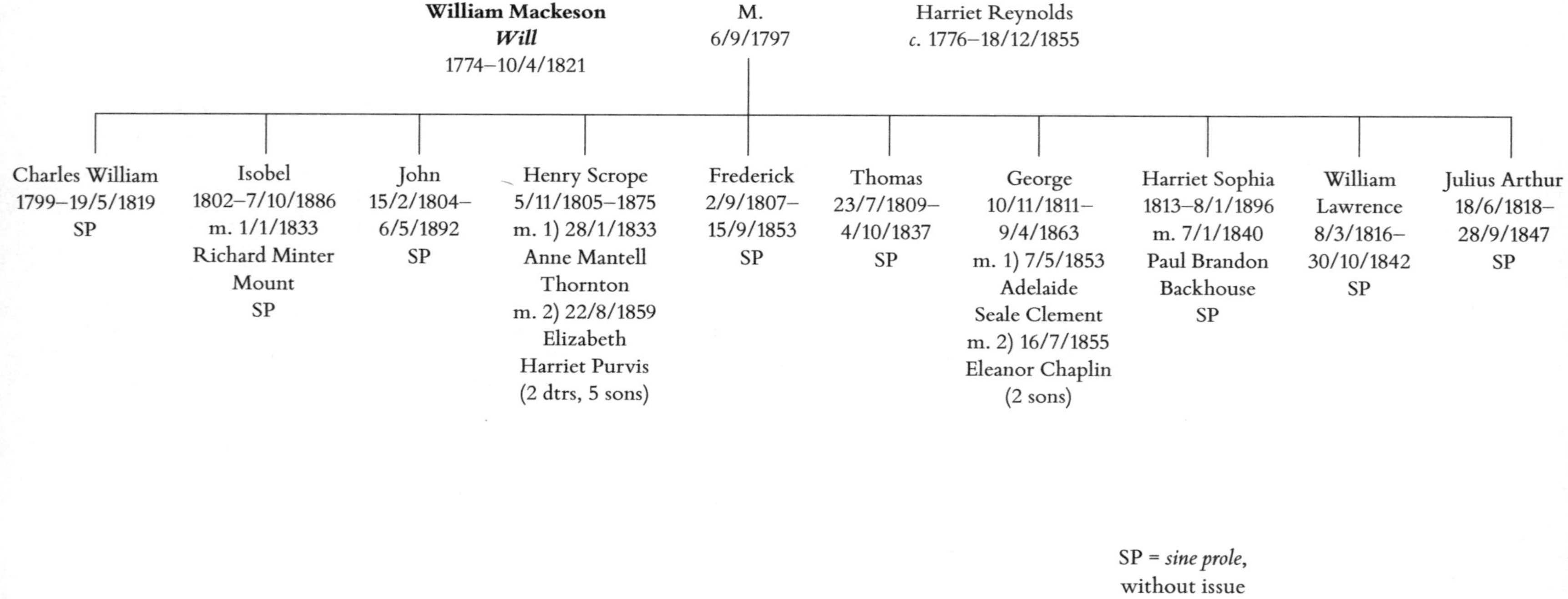

The descendants of Will Mackeson.

8

I Am Really Quite Tired Out

Will departed this life on 10 April 1821 at Bath, where he had probably been visiting his brother Jack, to whom he seems to have been close. It was Jack who arranged for the body to be removed to Hythe, for burial in St Leonard's church. This last journey took Will home, encased in a lead coffin, via Marlborough, Reading, Hammersmith, Wrotham and Ashford. The trip took two days, arriving in Hythe on Friday, 13 April. The funeral was five days later. Will was laid to rest in the newly built family vault, alongside his eldest son, Charles William, who had died two years earlier, aged 19.

The entrance to the Mackeson family vault beneath St Leonard's church in Hythe. *Author's collection*

The funeral over, probate had to be dealt with. Will had appointed Harry and two local businessmen as his executors. What they very soon discovered was that Will had died in debt. The probate accounts, drawn up in a book entitled 'Debts and Assets of William Mackeson' revealed that Will's assets had totalled £35,841 and his debts and encumbrances £32,706. This left a little over £3,000, which comprised effects that were an integral part of the brewery partnership and thus passed to Harry.[1] There was nothing left to support Will's widow, Harriet, and their nine children. None of the daughters were married and the sons were not yet employed.

Perhaps the worst of it was that Will had known that this would happen. The year before his death, he wrote to Jack, 'I much fear that in the event of my death, my poor children will be left in misery and distress', but neither he nor Jack shared the truth of his financial situation with the man who would have to deal with the mess, Harry.[2]

One of Harry's first actions was to give Will's oldest surviving son, 17-year-old John, a job in the brewery. He was put to work on the accounts.[3] It seems that this was an act of charity rather than a business need as by 1827 Peter Fisher was suggesting to Harry that it was time the young man found 'a situation in which he can support himself … as a Clerk in any Mercantile concern'.[4] This was achieved: John left the brewery the same year and worked for the rest of his life as an accountant in London.

Then Harry arranged for the education of the next four of Will's sons by placing them at the King's School in Canterbury. Henry Scrope (16 years old), Frederick (14), Thomas (12) and George (10) were all enrolled on 27 August 1821.[5] The school's fortunes had improved since the boys' uncle Philip was admitted there twenty-one years earlier and scholarships had become more competitive. They were admitted as 'Commoners' and their tuition fees were to be paid by their uncle Harry. Five-year-old William Lawrence and 3-year old Julius Arthur were left with their mother and sisters until they, too, were old enough to be admitted.

As well as his nephews' school fees, Harry had to find, and pay for, somewhere for them to lodge in Canterbury. Some cousins of his late mother, the Shrewsburys, lived in the city and may have been able to help out, though accommodating four schoolboys was not to be undertaken lightly.

Although Harry and Will had drawn up no formal partnership agreement, Harry had apparently no compunction in claiming the few assets that remained after Will's debts were paid. Had he not, the brewery could well have ceased trading, which would have been to no one's advantage. To ameliorate Harriet's situation Harry set up a legal partnership between himself, her and her children. This meant that they would receive a share of the profits. The original agreement has not been found, but its existence is verified by a deed of dissolution drawn up in 1847, shortly after the death of Will's youngest child, Julius Arthur.[6]

Out of his own pocket, Harry also paid off a mortgage of £800 that Will had taken out with George Shipdem, a prosperous sheep farmer and several times mayor of Hythe. These were generous acts on Harry's behalf and they kept Harriet and her children afloat, just. The executors of her husband's will wrote sternly to her:

> … but for a great sacrifice on the part of Mr Hy Mackeson and Mr Hammond you would find yourself entirely destitute. It will require all the fortitude you can command with a scrupulous and rigid economy.[7]

Harry was not off the hook, though. Will's children and assorted other family members harassed him endlessly for money. In 1830 he wrote to his stepmother, Clara, 'As God is my saviour, in consequence of the immense efforts I have made for poor William's family & the exigencies of the times as to business, I am exhausted.'[8]

At the same time, he was fretting about Philip's fatherless children, Clara's general fecklessness with money and his half-sister Kate's disastrous finances. Then in 1831, Isabel, Will's eldest daughter who had married a Canterbury solicitor, asked for more money. Harry replied that he could only spare £25 a month for 'every purpose whatever'.[9]

He went on to say 'my children work themselves from morning to night' just to keep the brewery going.

As he wrote this, Harry's only surviving son, Henry Bean, was just 18 years old. The other children were his four daughters, aged between 23 and 32. It seems that all of them worked for the family firm.

The role of women in family businesses is little understood because it is rarely documented and many women contributed to their family's income without being recognised as workers. On their very first day in the brewery in 1801, Harry and Will had paid one Mary Werger for nineteen pockets of hops, though no one of that name has been found as a hop grower or agent.[10] She was perhaps a daughter, sister, aunt or cousin who took on the role when there was no man to do it. A woman's economic role was part of her commitment to the family, the central unifying unit among the Victorian middle class. Just as a publican's daughters would work in the inn, and a grocer's daughters in the shop, so Harry's daughters worked in the brewery. There was plenty of work that did not involve hard labour. Harry's habit of keeping copies of all his extensive correspondence must have necessitated hours of scribing. Then there were orders to be made, invoices prepared, accounts to be settled, wages to be paid, stocktaking to be carried out, carriers to be arranged, letters and packets taken to and collected from the Post Office several times a day. The family home and servants and meals needed to be organised: their mother's health was always precarious, according to Peter Fisher's letters. It has been suggested that many of the women in families like the Mackesons had 'a mentality of self-subordination', though Elizabeth, Emma, Anne and Clara Mackeson may not have thought of themselves in this way.[11]

Having dealt with Isabel, Harry started to receive threatening letters from Thomas May, the younger of his half-sister Kate's sons by her first marriage, again, wanting money.[12] Harry wrote to Kate begging her intervention, but all she could offer was, 'I have endeavoured, my dear Harry, to extend my influence with my son, to persuade him to relinquish his claims on you, but without avail.'[13] Finally, in 1836, utterly exasperated, he wrote to Thomas May:

> Your calls are now so frequent it becomes necessary for me to state that it will be utterly impossible for me to answer them. Our business has fallen off to such a degree and I have sunk so much of my property in assisting so many of my relations in distress that I am really quite tired out.

He suggests that the young man finds work and starts saving. 'If you look around you and see the miserable state of tens of thousands you ought to be thankful for the small stipend which you at present enjoy.'[14]

All through the 1820s and '30s, Harry had been feeling huge commercial pressures. The local market for beer had declined: the number of troops at Shorncliffe was much reduced in the 1820s and the Royal Waggon Train was disbanded in 1833 followed by the Royal Staff Corps in 1838. England was also in the grip of the economic depression that had caused so much distress since the end of the Napoleonic Wars.

Harry had stopped brewing porter, but now found that there was a renewed demand for it in the town that was being met by William Marsh, the local pharmacist (and pastor of the Congregational Church in Hythe), who had invested in several butts of the beverage to sell in smaller casks in his shop.[15] He probably bought it from Barclay Perkins, whose agent advertised deliveries by hoy in the local press.[16] By 1829, Harry wrote that business was 'getting worse and worse and God only knows to what we shall at last be reduced'.[17]

The 1830s did not bring much good news of Will's family. John insisted on returning regularly to the brewery to check the accounts, in case Harry was swindling his family of their share of the profits. Harry then received reports in 1837 that John was consulting a solicitor about the partnership arrangement and that he had enlisted the support of the impecunious Thomas May.[18]

That same year, Harry received an urgent letter from his brother-in-law Peter Fisher, for his eyes only. He learned that Will's fifth son, Thomas, a lieutenant in the Royal Navy, had died aboard his ship in Malta 'in very melancholy circumstances'. 'He fell by his own hand, leaving, poor fellow, a paper expressing his hopes that this incumbrance would be removed from his Mother, Brothers and Sisters.'[19]

Fisher was clear that he would not divulge this to his family, but would maintain the fiction that Thomas had died after 'a short illness'. He was thwarted, though, by press reports of the inquest into the death, which appeared a month later.

Thomas's career in the navy had taken him from the Battle of Navarino in 1827, during the Greek War of Independence, to the surveying vessel HMS *Hecla* in April 1828. She sailed from Woolwich to West Africa to continue surveying the coastline there with a crew of eighty-eight. On her return, two years later, the complement was one acting captain, one carpenter, sixteen petty officers and seamen and four marines.[20] Most of the rest had died, but one acting lieutenant – Thomas Mackeson – had been invalided home after suffering from a fever. He had not been sent to convalesce with his family, but to a lunatic asylum.

A contemporary physician, Sir Gilbert Blane, thought that cases of insanity were seven times more common among sailors than among the general population. He blamed this on the frequency with which they got drunk and hit their heads on the ships' low beams. More recent studies of mental health issues in Royal Navy personnel in the eighteenth and nineteenth centuries have suggested more probable causes. Alcohol most likely played a large part, but so did trauma, diet, isolation and an excessively macho environment. Some men may have suffered from what is now known as post-traumatic stress.[21]

Whatever the cause of his 'insanity', Thomas was probably admitted to the Royal Navy's lunatic asylum at Haslar, Gosport, which had opened in 1818. It was based on the Retreat at York, a Quaker establishment that was the first to use 'moral management' as a treatment for insanity. A kindlier, more humane method, it rejected as far as possible the use of violence and restraints, common in other asylums.

There is often a lot of space between aspiration and reality. One report suggests that in the 1830s, when Thomas was there, the asylum was under the charge of a medical officer who held the view that lunacy could be cured or controlled only by the administration of severe disciplinary measures.[22] The treatment of the most famous 'lunatic' of the time was administered along these lines. It was reported of George III: 'His body was immediately encased in a machine which left no liberty of motion. He was sometimes chained to a stake. He was frequently beaten and starved.'[23] If the King of England could be treated like this, what hope was there for kindness for a lowly naval lieutenant?

It is not clear when Thomas returned to active service but in May 1834 he was appointed to HMS *Portland*. By October 1837 he had been in a bad way for some months, both mentally and physically. He could only carry out his duties occasionally. He had asked to be discharged and sent home. On the evening of his death, he retired to his cabin at about 7 p.m., lay down on his bunk and shot himself in the head with a rifle, using his foot on the trigger. In the note, he said that he feared being sent back to the asylum, where he had 'suffered much'.[24]

Although news of his nephew's suicide must have been distressing, Harry also had his immediate family and his livelihood to worry about. On the youngest of the family, Henry Bean Mackeson, rested Harry's hopes for the family business, but the young man could not decide whether to join his father in the brewery or take another path. In 1827, Peter Fisher wrote to Harry, 'If Henry shall be disposed to try the Navy in the Medical way, I will do my best towards securing him an assistant surgeon's appointment.'[25] Henry Bean was apparently not so disposed and around 1830 he was articled as a clerk to a solicitor, John Burt. Whether or not it was intended that he should himself become a solicitor or merely acquire a useful knowledge of the law, we don't know, but in the event, the brewery was his destiny.

Despite all this worry and activity, in 1831 Harry made his second foray into public life. His brother Tom had retired from the sea and was living in Hythe and both brothers applied for the Freedom of Hythe.[26] Harry could have done this years before as the qualifications were only that a man was resident and in possession of a freehold property worth at least £10. Then in 1836, both brothers stood as Conservatives in the election for town councillors. It was the first such election based on party political grounds. They did well and were near the top of the polling. There was, however, still a Liberal majority though the local press thought the Conservatives were 'greatly in the ascendant'.[27] They were wrong. The parliamentary constituency of Hythe was represented by Liberals from 1832 to 1895.

9

DINODOCUS MACKESONI

As a new decade started, Harry might have expected that he could take his ease a little more. He turned 70 in 1842 and was starting to suffer from the inconveniences and indignities of old age. He had to wear a truss. His brother-in-law Peter Fisher commiserated and, ever willing to offer medical advice, wrote to Harry, 'I wish only that your physician require on your part more caution perhaps in attending to keeping your Bowels open and take care not to attempt to be too Juvenile in your actions.'[1]

The town and the times Harry lived in had changed. The population of the country had doubled in the forty years since Harry and Will took on the brewery and the population of Hythe had kept pace, in 1833 having 2,287 residents.[2] Since the 1832 Reform Act it now returned only one MP to Parliament. The High Street looked different: it was still unlit at night (Hythe did not get a gas supply until 1851) but it now accommodated, as well as the usual trades, a confectioner, a hairdresser, a stationer, a bookbinder and a hat maker. There was obviously more money available to spend on non-essentials, though the theatre had closed its doors in 1837 as the military withdrew.

In place of the unpaid parish constables, there were now paid police officers, headed by a 'chief constable', John Friend, who combined the post with shoemaking. While there were several fee-paying schools, a new school for poorer pupils had been established in 1814 by the National Society for Promoting the Education of the Poor in the Principles of the Established Church in England and Wales (usually, for obvious reasons, referred to just as 'The National Society'). It was installed in a rather ramshackle house at the opposite end of the High Street from the brewery. Parents paid one penny a week to send their children there – but of course education was not yet compulsory.[3]

Travel, thanks to the railways, was becoming easier. In 1801, Richard Trevithick had built the world's first steam locomotive. Forty-two years later, Harry could travel by train from Folkestone to London in under three hours. Looking to the future, he and his brother Tom took shares in the Dover, Hastings and Brighton Railway Company, which was planning a coastal route to Exeter, avoiding London.[4] Tom became a director, along with his son Lumsden, the 'disappointing child' who was now a barrister. The railway came to nothing and the company was wound up, rather messily, ten years later.

Anglicans no longer had the sole place of worship in the town. William Marsh, the pharmacist, and his little congregation had built themselves a chapel in Back Lane, behind the High Street, and the Methodists were planning their own chapel in Prospect Road. Roman Catholics still had to wait another fifty years for their church.

The brewery was now well established and the money worries that had beset Harry in the past seemed to be easing. Will's children were adults. Harry continued to procure public houses – a recent acquisition was the George Tap in Rye. Even these had changed. Table service was becoming old-fashioned and drinks were now dispensed from a serving counter, or bar. On the bar was a hand pump, connected to a beer engine in the cellar below.

Occasionally, though, Harry's extended family still pestered him for money. His sister Mary wanted £5 to repay one of her children's debts without her husband knowing and, as he was then in Ireland, it was a good time to ask.[5] When her husband, Harry's close friend Peter Fisher died in 1844, Harry and his brother Tom dealt with the quarrelling Fisher offspring as to who inherited how much. William, one of the younger Fishers, who had received nothing from his father, wrote to Harry asking for a loan. William was notorious for defaulting on his debts and Harry was exasperated, 'I write this in a state of disgust, having just got a letter from Lt Fisher applying for a loan of £200 which I have neither the inclination nor the means to accommodate him with.'[6] Harry's solicitor (and the husband of his niece, Elizabeth Fisher), Martin Daniel of Ramsgate, had heard that William 'has gone and made a mess of it [...] for more than £300'. Six years later, William was still in debt and still complaining.[7]

Months before this, Harry had received news from Canterbury that his mother's cousin, Edward Shrewsbury, had died. Shrewsbury's son wrote, 'almost his dying words mean that I must write to you trusting that you will send a small sum of money to pay his last expenses'.[8] Even in their death throes, Harry's relatives seized one last opportunity to wring a little more cash from him.

Despite his occasional outbursts of exasperation, Harry's forbearance in the face of his family's demands upon him is admirable. Partly, this must have been because he saw himself as a patriarchal figure to his siblings, half-siblings, nephews and nieces and even distant cousins-in-law, with all that entailed. Partly, it may have been an effort to keep the family name respectable. It was 'respectable Connections' that had ensured Philip's acceptance as an apprentice attorney and, had he qualified, his professional status would have carried the cachet of social acceptability. Lacking any professional standing, Harry, a mere brewer, had to work harder to ensure his and his family's reputation.

By now, Harry was easing Henry Bean towards control of the business, though the younger man had been brought up with it and indeed still lived in the family home. The details of his education are lost to history, but as an adult he had a huge range of interests. At the age of 23, he gave a lecture to the Hythe Reading Society on 'Ornithology'.[9] Four years later, he was chairman of the group.[10] He was a member of the town's Harmonic Group.[11] He played cricket for the Hythe club and supported the Public Dispensary for the Benefit of the Poor. He also wanted to establish in the town a museum to display 'fossils, plants and natural curiosities'.[12] Fossils were one of his passions and he had the rare distinction of having found, in a quarry near Hythe, a hitherto unknown species. He discovered some limb and pelvic bones of what he thought at first was an iguanodon. It was not and was named for him, *Dinodocus Mackesoni*. The remains are still displayed in London's Natural History Museum. Partly as a result of this discovery, he was elected as a Fellow of the Geological Society in 1844.

He was consolidating his reputation in the town for honesty and reliability, and in 1846 acted as executor for James Nelson, a Scottish soldier turned innkeeper who had kept the appropriately named Nelson's Head public house in Hythe.[13]

By 1853, Henry Bean was carrying out most of his father's erstwhile business activities at the brewery and in family matters. That year, he wrote to his solicitor that William Fisher had yet again been asking for money but that he had refused to agree. He could not, he said, allow William's mother and sisters to 'sacrifice themselves for what you must admit is a mere momentary respite from William's inevitable fate'.[14]

Then, four years later, came a bombshell. Thirty-six years after Will Mackeson's death, his son John accused Harry of fraud in his execution of the will. Henry Bean wrote to Martin Daniel, 'I had fondly imagined we had finally wound up the affairs of my late uncle's estate – but the enclosed seems to re-open the matter.'[15] During his employment at the Hythe brewery, John had kept copious notes about the business accounts. After he left Hythe, Harry generously allowed him to return periodically to examine the books. Now John presented as 'evidence' of malpractice a mass of papers going back to Henry Mackeson's 1801 will and furthermore informed the Inland Revenue that Harry and Henry Bean were guilty of tax evasion. Their reaction can only be imagined.

There was a great deal of ill-tempered correspondence before Martin Daniel drew up a document setting out the facts of the case and exonerating the now 85-year-old Harry and his co-executors of any misdoing. A requirement of this was that Will's surviving children had to make statements to the effect that they accepted this decision.[16] The five still alive did so. The others had all met untimely ends.

After Thomas's suicide in 1837, his younger brothers William Lawrence and Julius Arthur both died of fever while in the service of the East India Company.

The fourth son, Frederick, also joined the East India Company, serving in the Bengal Native Infantry, but managed to avoid his brothers' fate. After a spell as political agent in the Punjab, he was sent to Peshawar, now in Pakistan, where he stayed during the First Anglo-Afghan War and where he earned a reputation as a first-class soldier and linguist. His next engagements were during the First and Second Anglo-Sikh Wars when notably, after the Battle of Chillianwala in 1849, he swam the treacherous Jhelum River to warn comrades on the other side of an imminent Sikh attack. That year he was promoted brevet lieutenant colonel.

He was then chosen for a special escort duty – accompanying the Koh-i-Noor diamond to England. The British had won the war and the diamond was ceded to Queen Victoria under the Treaty of Lahore (or stolen, depending on your point of view). On 1 February 1850, the jewel was sealed in a small iron safe inside a red dispatch box, both sealed with red tape and a wax seal, which for the sea voyage to England was placed inside a larger iron safe. It was a miserable trip. During a stopover at Mauritius, there was an outbreak of cholera on board and the locals threatened to open fire on the vessel unless it departed immediately. Back at sea it was caught in an enormous storm. Finally, on 1 July the diamond was handed over to the East India Company, who formally presented it to the queen two days later.

She did not much care for it, but nor did she much care for the East India Company: 'India should belong to *me*,' she wrote in her diary.[17] Its cut meant that the diamond did not sparkle and when viewed head on looked like a black hole. Prince Albert had it recut by Garrard, the royal jeweller. Now it was dazzling and the queen had it put in a circlet, but still did not like it. After Victoria's death, the stone was used in the crowns of the Queens Consort although Queen Camilla had it removed for her coronation in May 2023.

Frederick went back to India and was appointed Deputy Commissioner for Peshawar, where he was known by the locals as 'Kishin Kaka'. One evening in September 1853, as he was hearing appeals on his veranda, he was greeted with a salaam by a Muslim from Swat and

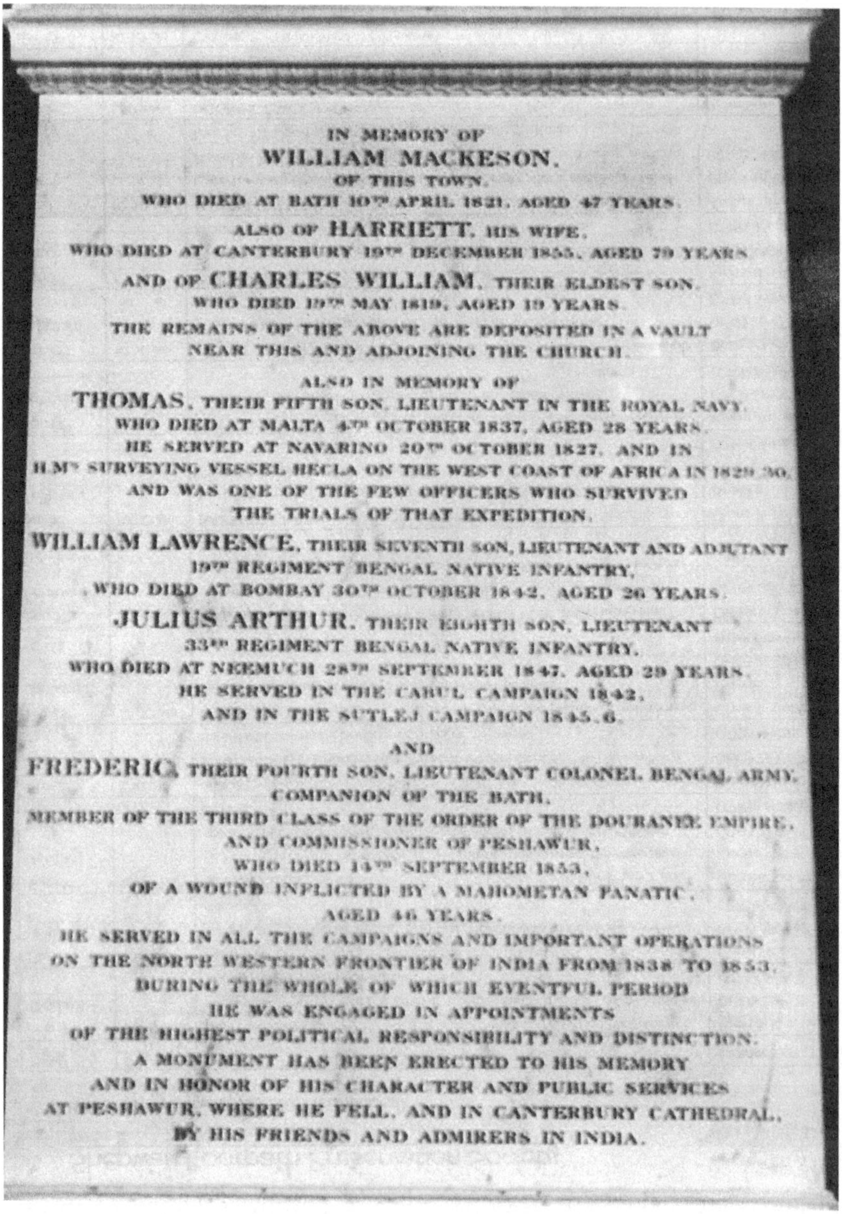

The memorial to the sons of William Mackeson in the Calvary Chapel at St Leonard's church, Hythe. *St Leonard's church*

presented with a piece of paper. The man then stabbed him. Frederick died four days later on 14 September. The assassin refused to speak and his motivation was assumed to be political, but rumours spread that this was, in fact, an honour killing. It was said that Frederick had become involved with a local woman. The Afghan code demanded that they both die. Frederick's commanding officer angrily dismissed this as a slander.[18] The assassin was hanged and his body wrapped in a pigskin (thus denying him entry to paradise) and burnt. Frederick is buried in Peshawar, not in the Christian cemetery, for fear of desecration, but in the Company Garden.[19] His name is on a memorial to Will's family in St Leonard's church, Hythe and he has a memorial of his own in Canterbury Cathedral. Both attribute his death to a 'Mahometan fanatic', to make matters absolutely clear.

Frederick is the first Mackeson for whom we have a physical description. He bucked the trend among officers of the Bengal Army for unkempt hair and bushy beards and had short, curly hair and 'a very elegantly curled moustache'.[20] He was also apparently a 'snappy dresser'.

Harry Mackeson died aged 87 on 9 March 1860. He had been a widower for nearly eight years, Mary Jane having been released from her sufferings on 1 November 1852 aged 81. Harry had outlived all but one of his siblings: only Mary Anne Fisher survived him. Harry's funeral and burial in the family vault were, at the family's request, strictly private, though the town had wanted the spectacle of a grand procession.[21] Still, the shops shut and a muffled peal was rung in the evening. The vicar of Hythe preached a funeral sermon to 'a crowded congregation' on the following Sunday evening.[22]

For nearly sixty years Harry had struggled to keep the brewery and his family afloat. He had dealt with economic depression, recession, war, lunacy, suicide, ingratitude, bankruptcies, a law suit, wastrel and importunate relatives, and premature deaths. Yet he passed on a thriving concern to a prosperous and respectable family. Arthur Clough's poem, written about 1847, could have been addressed to him:

For while the tired waves, vainly breaking
Seem here no painful inch to gain,
Far back through creeks and inlets making,
Comes silent, flooding in, the main.[23]

10

Many Songs Were Sung

At the time of his father's death, Henry Bean was still single and living with his parents at the age of 46. He had been disbarred from becoming a freeman of Hythe because he did not own his own home and was thus unable to vote, a decision he accepted with ill grace. It must have seemed to his friends that he was a confirmed bachelor. If so, he soon proved them wrong. Six weeks after the funeral he married Annie Adair Lawrie at the Manse in Monkton, Ayrshire. The service was performed by the bride's father, George James Lawrie DD, a presbyter of the Church of Scotland and minister of the parish. As was the norm in Scotland, Annie's wedding did not take place in the kirk but in a private house.

Ayrshire is a long way from Kent and it is something of a puzzle how the couple met. One solution might be another of Henry Bean's interests, game shooting. This has come to light because in 1836 he accidentally shot a boy in the face while out shooting partridge (he survived).[1] The unfortunate event did not, however, prevent his shooting licence from being renewed the next year. He shot with the Douglas brothers, Alex and Donald, the sons of the late Sir Kenneth Mackenzie, Baronet, and his wife Lady Rachel, who lived in Hythe.[2]

Sir Kenneth's family owned a crumbling castle and other land in Scotland, though his sons' wealth came from their mother. It may have been the case that the Douglas men spent time shooting in Scotland, that Henry accompanied them and that romance blossomed in the Highlands.

That April of 1860 was a busy month for the new groom. Three days after the ceremony he was nominated (presumably in his absence) as one of two churchwardens of St Leonard's in Hythe, which since 1844 had been a true parish church, separate from Saltwood. A few days later, he was at Herne Bay, explaining the geological features of the cliffs there to members of the East Kent Natural History Society. He also attended to his duties as the newly appointed commanding lieutenant of the Hythe Cinque Ports Volunteers, who had just received new rifles from the School of Musketry.[3] He soon persuaded the school's commanding officer, General Hay, to let the Volunteers have use of their shooting ranges on Saturday afternoons.[4]

The school had been established in Hythe in 1853, on land almost adjacent to the brewery. The name was a little misleading: the army was about to replace muskets with rifles and a dedicated school was thought necessary not only to train the men but also to study ways of improving the new weapon. Early instruction was in the new Minié rifle, which had the advantage of a reduced loading time. The initial course was held in June and by September of the following year a permanent staff was established. The plan was that each regiment in the British Army should send a party of ten men with an officer and NCO for a period of two months.

This renewed influx of soldiers to the town was good news for the brewery and a new public house (owned, of course, by the Mackesons) was opened next to the school to provide for them – the Ordnance Arms.

Shooting aside, Henry Bean also enjoyed the social aspect of the Volunteers. A meeting at the White Hart in 1861, ostensibly to consider the state of the accounts, became a 'very pleasant evening, in which many songs were sung' and at which 'the members did not disperse until rather a late hour'.[5] This was the first of many annual dinners. He also succeeded in making his Volunteers well known, and by 1864 had enrolled enough recruits to produce a full company: the 4th Company Cinque Ports Rifle Volunteers. Perhaps in recognition of this achievement, Henry Bean was promoted to captain two years later.[6]

Henry Bean was a very social animal, unlike his father, whose sole community event was the annual Christmas dinner he gave for his workforce at the Red Lion. His son continued the tradition, but had many other such commitments and was always happy to preside at ad hoc events, such as when a new landlord took over the Ship Inn at Dymchurch in 1860.

He was also now a member of the newly founded Kent Archaeological Society, which held its annual meeting in Hythe in 1862. Over two days, the assembled historians and archaeologists visited Saltwood Castle, St Leonard's church with its ossuary, Lympne, Lyminge and Westenhanger. Henry Bean played a full part in the proceedings – including, of course, the dinners – and displayed a spindle and distaff, a coin of Hadrian, a Merovingian gold coin and a ship's trumpet. The last item had been found on the beach at Romney and had 'passed into his hands', as, over the years, did many such finds.[7] He was becoming well known as a collector.

When the parvise (the room over the porch) of St Leonard's church was renovated in 1863, Henry Bean discovered therein piles of rotting historic documents, which he had moved to more suitable storage. Among them were records of St Leonard's church, which he used as a source to compile, with some help with the medieval Latin, a monologue on the Fraternity of the Assumption of the Blessed Virgin Mary at Hythe.[8]

Henry Bean was an early supporter of a railway connection for Hythe. The South-Eastern Railway Company (SER) had opened the line from London to Folkestone in 1843, but bypassed Hythe. The company claimed the town was served by the station at Westenhanger, but this was over 3 miles distant and most of that uphill. Years of lobbying finally resulted in a change of heart and the SER agreed to finance the purchase of land for a line. The Hythe and Sandgate Railway Company (HSRC), with Henry Bean as a director, was formed in January 1870.

The land purchase did not proceed smoothly and it was not until April 1872 that Prince Arthur of Connaught cut the first sod of the new railway. At the dinner for the great and good of Hythe that followed,

Henry Bean proposed the toast to the prosperity of the HSRC.[9] He was delighted with the new railway cutting as he was able to deliver an in situ lecture on the geological formation of the ground to fellow members of the Natural History Society.[10] He also acquired a number of bronze age artefacts that were unearthed during the excavation.

Hythe Station was opened on 9 October 1874 with much festivity, even though it was not, perhaps, what the town had envisaged. It was not central but up a steepish climb and had an unfortunate tendency to sink.[11] Nonetheless, there was parade of children from local schools carrying banners and a feast for them provided by Sir Edward Watkin, Hythe's recently elected MP and Chairman of the SER. Two triumphal arches were erected by the Coast Guard. The opening ceremony was performed by His Serene Highness the Duke of Teck (who had married a granddaughter of George III), the royal train passing through Hythe Station to the end of the line at Sandgate, a fifteen-minute journey,

Hythe Station in the snow in the 1890s, taken from an original glass negative. It closed in 1951. *Hythe Civic Society, Horton Collection*

and a special train bringing him back. Afterwards, a procession made its way down to the High Street. Henry Bean travelled in a carriage with the duke, Sir Edward and the mayor of Hythe. An 'elegant dejeuner' followed.[12] He was to rub shoulders with royalty again in 1881, when the Prince of Wales opened a new stretch of road along the seafront – named, of course, 'Prince's Parade'.

Somehow, among all this activity, Henry Bean found time to gather rainfall data for the Royal Society; to contribute to a history of the weald of Kent;[13] to keep a nature diary; to run 'penny rambles', where he delivered field lectures on local flora and fauna;[14] to become an alderman and deputy mayor; to continue his work as a churchwarden; to become a trustee of St Bartholomew's Hospital in Hythe;[15] to breed fancy chickens (Dorkings);[16] and to run the brewery.

The business was doing well. As was the norm for breweries, the Mackesons measured their output in terms of quarters of malt brewed. In 1875 this was 2,777 quarters and the figure rose steadily.[17] Their employees seem to have been loyal. One newspaper report of the annual dinner comments that 'the same faces are seen every year'.[18] It must be assumed that Henry Bean was a good employer paying a decent wage.

The elements that combined to make a success of the business were complex. There were now several locations to be managed, as stores had been established at Ashford, Rye, Hastings and Canterbury to facilitate deliveries across east Kent and Sussex.[19] Deliveries required drays, carts and wagons, and these required horses to pull them. The horses required feeding. The Mackesons' animals were well fed on clover, sanfoin, oats, beans, bran, peas and rye grass. They also needed stabling and servants to look after the stables. There were vets' bills, too, and bills from the farrier for shoeing, but the beasts generated a small income from the sale of manure to local gardeners.[20] Despite this, expenditure on horses was one of the brewery's bigger outgoings and they were more expensive than its labourers.

The biggest outgoings, however, were still for barley and hops. Henry Bean's main supplier for the latter was now Wood, Field and

Hanbury, a hop merchant based in London.[21] Hop cultivation was by then decreasing in Kent in favour of fruit.

Apart from the actual brewing process, there were casks to be made and maintained. Coopering was a skilled trade and an apprentice learned how to make casks of all sizes from oak staves, how to 'pickle' them (boil them in water) and hoop them. He also knew how to clean 'a stinker' (a contaminated cask), how to 'cobble' a leaky one (mend it) and how to piece it through (enlarge it). Having learned all this, his new status as a cooper was celebrated by stuffing him into a barrel and covering him in a mixture of water, beer, soot, ash and whitewash. This rite of passage endured at the Hythe brewery until the 1960s.[22]

Then there was the paperwork attendant on all business operations, including licences to be renewed for the public houses and insurance policies to be negotiated. Wages and salaries had to be paid and accounts settled for the purchase of such necessary items as malt shovels, coal

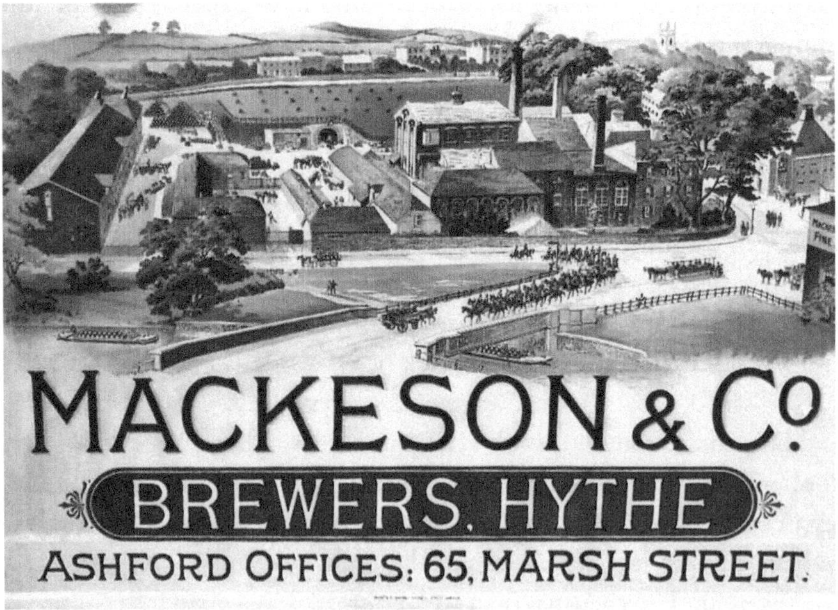

A brewery advertisement showing the original malthouse at far right and the new building at far left. *Author's collection*

buckets, bungs, brooms, mops, horse cloths, spiles and shives (types of cask bung), a wash stand for the office, a thermometer, wax vestas (matches), wooden shoes, sulphite of lime, pectic acid, candles and squeegees (not the modern version with a rubber blade for window cleaning but a tool with a leather or wood edge for scraping floors and other mucky surfaces).

In the 1870s, as the Industrial Revolution marched on, there were innovations. Gas lamps were installed and the coopers' job made easier by the purchase of a 'patent cask washer'. A new steam boiler was put in together with a steam pump. A second malthouse was built on land bought from St Leonard's church and the road around it was tarred.[23]

The Mackesons' income was not just from the beer they brewed. The business also sold small quantities of other brewers' and distillers' products. There was a rental income from the public houses and from cottages owned by the family. Some of these were used to house its own workers and there were others, mostly inherited from John Friend, scattered about the Romney Marsh.

Henry Bean also managed the agricultural lands that had come into the family through inheritance. It seems that he used at least some of these for grazing sheep, as he operated fell-mongering pits in Hythe, near the source of the brewery's water.[24] Here wool was removed from sheepskins by soaking them in water and sodium sulphide, a malodorous business. Other acreage was leased, providing a rental income.

The brewery's needs created work for local men and jobs for the traders of Hythe. As well as those working in the brewery and at fell-mongering, the Mackesons used casual labour, men and boys, for odd jobs. One of the boys was John Fryer, who earned part of his school fees by working at the brewery. Forty years later, he was the University of California's first Professor of Oriental Language and Literature. The established Hythe firms were used for more specialised work. Finnis and Ronalds of the High Street provided upholstery for the offices; Worthington & Co., coachmakers, provided carts and carriages.

As well as the many public houses he owned, Henry Bean had signed a contract with the War Office to run five military canteens at

Shorncliffe Barracks. He erected the wooden huts and paid a ground rent of 4*s* a year and sublet the buildings to contractors at £104 per annum. He had the monopoly on supplying beer. This arrangement, although clearly profitable for the brewery, was not universally popular among the 2,000-odd troops now in residence at Shorncliffe, who preferred the system in place at other military establishments where each regiment had responsibility for its own canteens. There were mutterings in the press that suggested that Henry Bean was profiteering.[25]

By 1865, the War Office had decided that the regimental system was the way forward and that 'where possible', the canteens should be managed in this way, but stopped short of evicting sitting tenants.[26] This was just a stay of execution and Henry Bean was in 1868 given notice to quit by the end of March.[27]

His major concern at this time was the water supply to the brewery, which did not match demand. In 1866, like his father before him, he went to the Town Council. He asserted that he had first claim on the town's water supply laid on by Harry and Will in 1804. So many years had passed since this event that the rest of the council were unaware of the arrangement. Henry Bean enlightened them and pointed out that he did not work his fell-mongers' pits in summer as otherwise 'the town would not have a teapot full of water'.[28]

The Town Clerk did some digging in the archives and found that Henry was correct, but still the council quibbled until in January 1868, it finally agreed to his request for a better supply to the brewery and to Henry's private dwelling.[29] The work carried out at the Dentalls comprised a reservoir built in one of Henry Bean's fell-mongering pits and a dividing weir to control the flow of water. The whole was contained in rather a fine structure that is now, thanks to the efforts of local historians, Grade II listed.

11

Dae Ye Mind O' Lang, Lang Syne

Henry Bean lived with his growing family at The Elms at the western end of Hythe High Street. A son, yet another Henry, was born in May 1861, with announcements made in national newspapers in England and Scotland. Twin daughters followed in 1863 and another three daughters and a son joined the family in the next ten years. All these children needed to be educated and fitted for the life to which the Mackesons aspired.

Young Henry was at Uppingham School by the time he was 9 years old and was joined there later by his brother George. The school was then under the headmastership of Edward Thring, a remarkable educator, who had taken control in 1853 of a small grammar school with three masters and forty pupils and transformed it into a highly respected public school with nearly 500 boarders.[1] These boys were mostly the sons of manufacturers, merchants, doctors and clergymen, and perhaps significantly, several Brighton brewers.

The education Thring provided would, he intended, inculcate 'duty and honour and grit', which he believed were the qualities of true manliness. He provided a broad-based education, including science, together with music, gardening, carpentry, nature study and sport. Cricket was the summer sport of choice and in 1872, Thring appointed a cricket professional to the school.[2] Two years later, Uppingham appeared at Lord's against the MCC for the first time. This introduction to the game left a lasting impression on both Henry Bean's sons, especially George.

The Elms at the end of Hythe High Street. It has now been extended, converted into apartments and renamed The Maltings. *Author's collection*

Their sisters were all educated at home. A government commissioner, reporting on the state of education in England in the 1860s, noted that among the middle classes, 'boys were educated for the world, girls for the drawing room'.[3] Henry Bean's daughters would not, as his sisters had, work in the family business, but would acquire the 'gentler graces and winning qualities which will be their best passports to marriage'.[4]

Henry Bean had financial obligations towards his four maiden sisters, who had contributed so much to the early success of the brewery. After their father's death and the introduction of the new Mrs Mackeson to the family home, they had been set up in their own establishment in Hythe, complete with a cook and housemaid. Although their father had provided for them in his will, their brother also established a loan account of £650 with the brewery's bank on which they could draw for unexpected expenses.[5]

Elizabeth, the eldest sister, died while visiting Tunbridge Wells in 1862. The women enjoyed visiting spa towns and also spent time in Buxton and Cheltenham. Her sisters moved to another house in Saltwood, quieter than Hythe with professional people as neighbours. Emma and Clara died in the 1880s, both aged over 80; Anne outlived all her siblings, dying in 1896.

Henry Bean was not troubled by his extended family in the way in which his father had been. His surviving Mackeson cousins – the children of his uncle Will – were by the 1860s comfortably settled. Will's eldest son, John, had finally accepted that he could squeeze no more money out of his uncle Harry Mackeson and went back to accountancy and London. His siblings seem to have acknowledged, at least in public, that no injustice had been done. They lived respectably enough: Henry Scrope was a Canterbury physician and the father of Charles, who took holy orders and became something of a celebrity priest. George was a civil servant, while Isabel married a solicitor in Canterbury Cathedral and died childless in 1886. Her younger sister Harriet Sophia married an army chaplain, travelled with him to Agra and lost him to fever eight months after their wedding. She returned home and lived latterly with her sister.

Henry Bean's Fisher cousins prospered. Even the improvident William had got married and settled in Walmer. Two of Jack Mackeson's children achieved some public renown. The successful career as a QC of William Wyllis Mackeson meant that his name was in the London papers weekly and he published works on mortgage law. His brother, Frederick Laing Mackeson also attracted press attention for his exploits as a lieutenant colonel in North-West India, though his death in 1874 seems to have been due to natural causes. The children of Tom Mackeson and of Elizabeth Parkinson favoured the professions or the army. Thomas May, Kate's son, who had pestered Harry endlessly for money, eventually became a successful barrister. He died in 1862 and left his brother Henry £50, a quantity of silver plate and 'such furniture as my Trustees may think fit for him to furnish a house'.[6] Whatever Henry May did with the inheritance, it was not used to furnish a house and, in his 70s, he lodged in a beer house in Wheathampstead, Hertfordshire, claiming spuriously to be a retired sea captain.

When extended family arrived on the Mackeson doorstep, it was from another direction. In November 1877 Henry Bean and Annie were joined in Hythe by Annie's parents, George James Lawrie, the former presbyter of Monkton, Ayrshire, and his wife Laura Louisa, who were both now in their 80s.[7]

With them were three grandchildren. Annie's sister Flora had married Thomas Shelford, merchant and up-and-coming politician, in Singapore on Christmas Eve 1867. Thomas, known to friends as 'Tim' and his brother, the Rev. Leonard Shelford were also good friends of Henry Bean.[8]

In the five and a half years of her marriage, Flora gave birth to six children before expiring on a visit to her parents in Monkton in 1873. The younger three of these offspring moved to live with their grandparents and a governess in Elm House in Hythe. (Elm House was the former home of Lionel Lukin, inventor of the lifeboat and is not to be confused with The Elms.) Their father, Thomas Shelford, stayed in Singapore.

George Lawrie's quiet life in Monkton had hidden a rather more adventurous past. The eldest son of another minister, he had won an Exhibition to the University of Glasgow, where he became a Doctor of Divinity. He then sailed for India and became a presbyter of the Church of Scotland at St Andrew's Church, Madras (now Chennai) in November 1823.

He was presbyter-in-charge from 1824 to 1839, but evidently found time to travel about the sub-continent and to meet Laura Louisa Ludlow, the second daughter of Samuel Ludlow F.R.C.S., Residency Surgeon of Delhi. Her family lived there in a house built by her father, so grand it was locally nicknamed 'Ludlow Castle'. The couple were married in Calcutta.

Back in Madras, George and a colleague founded a school for boys, which originally had fifty-nine pupils, but has since expanded to become Madras Christian College, with a 365-acre campus and a huge student population. Laura returned to Scotland in about 1839, with her two daughters, including the future Annie Adair Mackeson, who was born at sea. George re-joined his family there to take up the incumbency at Monkton. Both his father and grandfather had been literary friends of Robert Burns, and George wrote, too, publishing *Songs and Miscellaneous Pieces*. In 1887 his poetry was used in *Modern Scottish Poets*. He is credited with having written the song 'Dae ye mind o' lang, lang syne': the first verse (of many) follows. It is to be sung to the tune of 'John Peel'.

Do ye mind the sunny braes
Whaur we gathered hips and slaes,
And fell among the bramble busses,
Tearin' a' our claes;
And for fear they would be seen
We gaed slippin' hame at e'en,
But were licket for our pains in the morning.

George died of 'natural decay' in Hythe aged 82 in 1878, not long after his arrival in the town; Laura lived to be 91, living latterly with her daughter and son-in-law in their new residence, Hillside House. The couple are buried together in St Leonard's churchyard.

The new house, not far from the brewery, had a wide drive for carriages leading off Bartholomew Street. It came with an acre and a half of garden.[9] There, Henry Bean built greenhouses and installed a vinery, or to be more exact, his gardener John Hewett, did. In moving there, and no longer living 'over the shop', Henry Bean and Annie Mackeson were making a clear statement about the way in which they now saw their position in Hythe society. As well as a gardener, they had a live-in cook, housemaid and nurse, the latter was probably to care for Annie's mother.

Harry and Will had been the first of the Mackeson clan to live in Hythe and as well as their burial vault, Henry Bean wanted a more significant memorial. He decided on a window in St Leonard's church, in a lancet of the great east window, above the altar. 'Richly and tastefully painted', it depicted the nativity and the childhood of Jesus and was created by Michael O'Connor and Sons of London.[10] Their work was well thought of and still is for its clarity and unfussiness. Unfortunately, the entire east window was destroyed by enemy action in 1940.

At around the time the window was commissioned, Henry Bean also arranged for a wall plaque in the church to commemorate his two dead sisters. The first, Mary Jane, had died aged 5 in 1809, four years before Henry Bean was born. The other was his eldest sister, Elizabeth.

12

In Every Sense a Gentleman

Despite all his interests, Henry Bean kept a firm hand on the rudder of the brewery. The 1881 census shows that he was employing thirty-six men. These included a head brewer (paid £87 a year), a head maltster, George Adams, and Thomas Eley, a travelling representative, with a basic salary of £112 plus generous expenses and commission.[1] With this level of income, Eley and his wife could afford a live-in servant.[2] Stephen Godden, the chief clerk and cashier, who joined the firm in 1871, had a salary of £200 ten years later.[3] Godden had grown up next door to the brewery. His father, another Stephen, was employed as an engine driver there and the family lived in one of the cottages Henry Bean leased for his employees. Godden was obviously a bright boy and at 13 years old was a pupil-teacher at Hythe's National School. Now, widowed, he and his son lived in a smart villa in the new Park Road development in Hythe. He stayed with the brewery until 1911, becoming company secretary, by which time he had moved to an eight-room house in Earls Avenue with his new family.

Richard Lee was another long-term employee. He started 'as a lad' with the brewery in the 1860s, working as a clerk. He eventually became foreman, supervising all the outside work until his retirement after forty-one years.[4] He worked alongside his brother-in-law Robert Keith, formerly a quarter-master at the nearby School of Musketry. Another employee, Daniel Brett, a cellarman at the brewery, was able to use his expertise and connections to take on the licence of the Nelson's Head, a Mackeson public house, in 1882.

Some employees, inevitably, were not pillars of the community. In 1875, a drayman, William Marden, was charged with embezzlement. He had been taking money from customers to whom he delivered but not remitting the whole amount to his employer. It was Stephen Godden who picked up the discrepancy.[5] A decade later, the manager of the Ashford store, Edward Fordred, disappeared. On examination, his account books were found to be works of fiction. Two years later he returned to his wife in Folkestone, saying he had been in America. He was arrested, charged with embezzlement and sentenced to three months' hard labour.[6]

The houses Henry Bean rented to his employees were leased from the Trustees of St Bartholomew's Hospital, major landowners in the area. There were six dwellings, one vacant in 1881 following the death of Stephen Godden senior, the others occupied by James Wells, a foreman, his wife and six children; Edward East, a married drayman with five children; a younger couple, William and Rosina Adams with a daughter and Adams's widowed mother; Frederick Booth, brewery labourer, with his wife and two children; and a retired labourer, Henry Dray, a widower. The cottages were tiny – besides the kitchen, there were only three rooms – but not unusually so for the period.

In 1881 Henry Bean offered to buy the properties, but was thwarted by the Charity Commission, which refused to countenance the sale. Henry Bean was a good tenant and the rent was secure, so there would be no benefit to the hospital.[7] They relented a few years later.[8]

The brewery now laid on for its employees an annual excursion to London by train with two special saloon coaches attached to the service for their exclusive use. In 1887 they particularly enjoyed the American Exhibition at Earl's Court with 'Buffalo Bill's Wild West'.[9]

Young Henry, aged 19, was also on the payroll. After his schooling at Uppingham had finished, he had spent some time studying chemistry – a useful subject for a brewer – in Edinburgh. Now he had joined the family firm and on the 1881 census is described as a brewer. He was paid £200 a year.[10]

Towards the end of the nineteenth century, brewery profits in England were often static or declining. Beer consumption peaked in 1878 and then fell rapidly.[11] Competition came from the increasing availability of tea and coffee as well as safe drinking water, and breweries and public houses were vilified by a vociferous temperance movement. In Hythe, this included the Band of Hope, founded in 1879; a Temperance Hall was in place by 1886 and was followed by a Temperance Hotel in the High Street.

Matters were not helped by Gladstone's 1872 Licensing Act. This created a raft of alcohol-related offences. For the first time it was an offence to be drunk in a public place or drunk in charge of a horse, a carriage, a loaded firearm or (rather oddly) a cow. Public houses could shut no later than midnight and licensing hours would be decided by the local authority and enforced by the police. The law also now stated that magistrates could immediately remove the licence from premises where the law had been broken. Hythe magistrates had no compunction in implementing the new laws. In 1876, they penalised fourteen men and women for being drunk and disorderly.[12] The next year it was thirty-nine. One of these, William Daisy was charged with being drunk in charge of a horse and cart and also of assaulting Henry Bean, who declined to press charges.[13]

Faced with these impediments, Henry Bean's expansion of the business was cautious. A new store at Eastbourne was opened in 1880[14] and was followed by another in Sittingbourne in 1886.[15] At about the same time, the business took over a brewery in Tontine Street, Folkestone, variously known as the Imperial or Atlas. It came with sixteen public houses to add to the Mackeson estate at a total cost of £16,750. Henry Bean closed the brewing works, but continued to use the buildings as offices and a bottle store and kept open the adjoining licensed premises, the Brewery Tap.[16] This was becoming a common move by brewers across the country, as it increased the number of tied houses while reducing the brewing competition. Henry Bean went on to acquire the Three Mariners and the Oak, both in Hythe, and invested in building land on West Parade, Hythe and in Saltwood.[17]

The Brewery Tap in Tontine Street, Folkestone, with decorative tiled panels. *Author's collection*

In addition to bitters and stouts, the brewery had started producing 'Anglo-Lager ale'. This was not a true lager as it is known today, but had a lower alcohol content and was popular in the export market. The brewery advertised this and all its wares in the local press and, in common with other retailers, used other media, too. There was a board at Hythe Station, posters at branches of W.H. Smith at other, bigger, stations; business cards to hand out to customers and contacts; and corporate gifts bearing the Mackeson name, including paper knives.[18]

Away from the brewery, Henry Bean was making a name for himself in local politics. He was elected mayor of Hythe for an unbroken run of nine years, from 1872 to 1880, before insisting that it was time he stood down. During this time, he acted as Speaker of the Cinque Ports during an Annual Brotherhood and Guestling, by now a largely formal gathering of civic dignitaries from the ports. After his resignation as mayor, he continued as an alderman and JP almost until his death.

In the 1880s he took on another challenge, this time in his role as churchwarden of St Leonard's. Restoration of the rather dilapidated church had started in 1875 under the direction of the vicar, who had raised £10,000 for the work. It continued in 1887, with a new architect, John Pearson, who had designed Truro Cathedral. The aim was to complete the church with many of the features intended by its medieval creators, who had been stalled when the town's wealth as a Cinque Port dried up. Five centuries after it was started, the vaulting to the chancel and aisle roofs was completed and a pulpit, with fine Venetian mosaic work, installed. A lot of the administrative work for this undertaking, including fundraising, fell to the churchwardens.

Henry Bean's children were now mostly adults. Young Henry and George were learning the ropes of running the business, with the inevitable mishaps along the way. In 1887, accompanied by George Adams, who had been the brewery's head maltster for forty-five years, Young Henry bought some barley at Ashford. When it arrived at Hythe it smelt bad and he refused to take delivery or to pay. The suppliers sued. The Mackesons lost.[19] It was, however, a sign that Henry Bean was allowing his sons to make mistakes and learn from them. Increasingly, he left them to manage the business.

Young Henry also followed in his father's and grandfather's footsteps in military matters, joining the Volunteer Battalion of East Kent Regiment the Buffs as a subaltern in 1880.[20] Commissioned as a lieutenant, he was promoted to captain in 1884.[21]

The elder of his twin sisters, Laura, was in 1888 engaged to be married to the Rev. John Algernon Sidgwick, whom she had met while he was curate at Saltwood.[22] They were married in April that year, in a no-expense-spared extravaganza that displayed the Mackesons' wealth. The local press reported that the bride's dress was 'of a very rich and costly nature as also were the bridesmaids' and 'the church was filled with one of the largest and most brilliant assemblies it has ever contained'.[23] A ball was held in the town hall in the evening: the venue was described as 'looking like a fairyland'.

Perhaps at the behest of his cricket-loving sons, Henry Bean got up a cricket team in the summer of 1885, 'Mr Mackeson's Eleven', in which, of course, Young Henry and George played. George was already joint secretary of Hythe Cricket Club, with which he remained associated until his death. He was not the only cricketing Mackeson: one of Will's grandsons, William James Mackeson, was a first-class cricketer, playing for the MCC in 1882.

It was George who married next, in 1893, but not in Hythe. He wed Carlota Jenoveva Abel in Chelsea. Carlota had been born in Chile, the daughter of John Sangster Abel, a British émigré, and Jenoveva Recabarren. Orphaned young, she and her siblings were brought to the UK and adopted by their childless uncle, Sir Frederick Abel, Baronet, a chemist and the inventor of cordite. Carlota and her sister had been regular visitors to Hythe, by then a popular, but quite genteel, seaside resort.[24]

The simple grave stones of Henry Bean Mackeson, his son George and his father-in-law George Lawrie, who lie with their wives in St Leonard's churchyard. *Author's collection*

At 4.30 on the afternoon of 26 February 1894, Henry Bean Mackeson died.[25] The local press said of him:

> He was in every sense a gentleman, genial, courteous, just, esteemed by his equals and respected by those in humbler walks of life. He was charitable without ostentation [...] he was in every sense, with his family, the leader of social life in Hythe.[26]

He was buried, not in the family vault, but outside in the graveyard. He was joined there when the time came by his wife and by their daughter Mildred. George and his wife Carlota lie alongside.

He had, in his will, set up a trust fund for his daughters, with the Shelford brothers as trustees. He gave £100 to his coachman, and the family pictures and plate to Young Henry. The residue went to his wife during her lifetime and the brewery business to Young Henry and George.[27]

13

THE POWER WAS A HORSE

When Young Henry and George took over their father's business, they embarked on a programme of modernisation, investment and expansion.

They started to buy land again, something the family had not done for some time. This was not, however to lease to graziers or farmers or to use themselves, but for building. Hythe was expanding fast, towards the sea on the old 'inned' land, westward across the Romney Marsh, to the east towards Folkestone and up the hill towards the village of Saltwood. The Mackesons bought building land along the Dymchurch Road, in Saltwood itself and further afield, in Whitstable, Herne Bay, Canterbury, Folkestone and Dover.[1] Land that they already owned was sold off in parcels to builders. The Dentalls field, north of the High Street, comprised about 5 acres and was advertised as having 'magnificent sea views to east and west'.[2] The first plot went to Robert Worthington, head of the local coachbuilding family, who built himself a six-bedroom house on the corner plot, from which he also had a magnificent view of his works.

The Mackesons had building plans of their own. The most ambitious was a new hotel near the railway station in Herne Bay.[3] A sparsely populated fishing village at the beginning of the nineteenth century, the town was now a popular seaside destination with a mile-long parade and large assembly rooms, and was soon to boast one of the longest piers in England. The Grand Hotel in Station Road, described as 'luxuriously appointed', was formally opened on 1 July 1899 with a luncheon for local dignitaries.[4]

Another achievement was a new malthouse in the parish of St Stephen in Canterbury.[5] Built in 1898 to 1899, it has been described as 'the ultimate in floor malting design'.[6] It was a four-storey building with storage at two levels and growth floors on three storeys. There was an internal elevator to take sprouted barley to the kiln floor. Barley was brought in by rail to a sidings at the rear of the building, where it was hoisted to storage space at roof level. The resultant malt was also moved to Hythe by rail. The Mackeson brothers' father and grandfather, both great proponents of the railway, would have been delighted. There were also four terraced cottages for the maltsters on site, because the barley had to be watered day and night, and the temperature checked every six hours.

Back in Hythe, the brewery was upgraded with the latest technology, including dressing machines, carbonators and mechanical bottle fillers. To make life easier in the office, a telephone (number: Hythe 7) and radiators were installed.

William Bennett, an employee who retired in the 1930s, later recalled working conditions in the 1890s. He started at the brewery aged 18 in 1893 and was paid 18*s* for a sixty-hour week – a foreman got £1 6*s* 6*d*. These rates were broadly in line with the wages of industrial workers elsewhere in the country. The only holidays were bank holidays and the annual excursion to London. He worked in the mill, which was 'in a cone-shaped building. There was a shaft projecting out of the building and the power was a horse.' The racking room, he remembered 'had not a window anywhere, the only illumination coming from a small gas-jet. Overhead were heavy oak beams, much too low for me to work without stooping.'[7] This was undoubtedly uncomfortable and unpleasant, but at a time when coal miners worked ten-hour shifts in the dark, bent double, it was not regarded by the factory inspectors as unacceptable.

However, it was not the working conditions of the brewing staff that were immediately improved. In 1899, the Mackesons started building new office accommodation adjoining The Elms on what had previously been the entrance to the works.[8]

For Young Henry, emerging from the long shadow of his father, this was a new start in life in more ways than one. In 1891 he had been terribly injured when on parade with the Buffs at Canterbury. His horse reared, threw him and then fell on him, causing abdominal and lower limb injuries.[9] He was taken to the Kent and Canterbury Hospital, where he was to remain for six months, the family sending their own physician, Dr Osborne, to oversee his treatment. They even moved temporarily into the rectory at Harbledown to be near him.

When Young Henry was finally discharged in January 1892, he travelled home to Hythe by train in a specially constructed ambulance carriage. To make the journey from the station as painless as possible, straw was laid in the ruts in the roads. His father sent a cheque for £100 to the hospital, in gratitude for their care, and the church bells rang a special peal.[10]

His convalescence was protracted, but a year later he could take short walks with two sticks.[11] Because some of the shattered bone had been removed from his leg, he walked with a pronounced limp for the rest of his life.

For the first year after Henry Bean's death, Young Henry carried on his father's meteorological measurements and kept a weather diary, but there is nothing to indicate he kept this up.[12] He also, like his father, became a churchwarden at St Leonard's in Hythe in 1894, was politically active, and chaired Conservative Association meetings to choose a parliamentary candidate.[13] The Association supported Sir Edward Sassoon's successful bid to become the town's MP. Sir Edward was actually a Liberal Unionist, but members of his party had formed a coalition with the Conservatives and the two parties amalgamated in 1905.

In 1895 Young Henry married Ella Cecile Ripley of Surbiton, the daughter of a foreign exchange broker and member of the London Stock Exchange. She was an expert horsewoman, specialising in driving tandems. He gave his bride a diamond and gold necklace and they honeymooned on the fashionable French Riviera, the resort of the leisured rich. On their return to Hythe, brewery employees unhorsed their carriage and drew it to Hillside House.[14]

The couple's stay at the family home was short. Within a few weeks, they had moved to Augusta Gardens in Folkestone and Young Henry declined to be reappointed as a churchwarden as he no longer lived in the parish.[15] He hoped to return, he said.[16] He never did and he and Ella soon moved permanently to St Olave's in Trinity Crescent, Folkestone. It was the beginning of the end of the long association between the Mackeson family and Hythe.

Augusta Gardens and Trinity Crescent offered smarter, more stylish houses than were to be found in Hythe. St Olave's had seventeen rooms and required a live-in staff of six to maintain it and the family. Folkestone itself offered far grander society than was to be encountered in Hythe. May Solly-Flood, almost exactly the same age as Ella and an inveterate payer of calls and leaver of visiting cards, called only three times on the Mackesons during her thirteen years in Hythe.[17] Mrs Deedes at Saltwood Castle, Lady Maria Fitzclarence in Augusta Gardens and the Brockmans at Beachborough were favoured, as were titled visitors to Folkestone such as Lady Wigan, Lady Hardinge and Lady D'Aquilar. These people were, like May, untainted by any association with trade and if they were wealthy, it was through 'old money', inherited, not earned. May's father was a distinguished general, Sir Frederick Solly-Flood, of the Anglo-Irish landed gentry. The Solly-Flood family were not wealthy, but that was not of the greatest importance. What really mattered were connections, land and pedigree.

Young Henry and his new wife did not yet have these, but they were working on it. At St Olave's they counted among their neighbours Vice Admiral Charles Cooper Penrose-Fitzgerald, who in 1914 was responsible for starting the white feather campaign against men not in uniform; Ralph Pelham Nevill, son of an earl and former High Sheriff of Kent; Sir William Carington, ex-soldier, ex-MP and still Keeper of the King's Privy Purse; and Alfred Chase Parr, a retired admiral and formerly aide-de-camp to Edward VII. These were men with influence and friends in high places. Young Henry was elected to London's exclusive Carlton Club, which, although no longer functioning as the central office of the Conservative Party, was still the venue for key political discussions and was where the 1922 Committee was formed.

Young Henry's move to Folkestone left Henry Bean's widow alone in the big house with her two remaining unmarried daughters, Annie and Mildred. In 1894 Mary, the younger of the twin daughters, had married Richard Henry Green, a ship builder, and gone to live with him in Haslemere, Surrey. On the same day, the youngest girl, Elizabeth (usually called Elspeth), had married Arthur Moubray, farmer and former army officer, of Sellindge. There had been an evening reception at Hillside House at which Hythe Town Band played and were delighted to be given wedding cake.[18] George and his wife Carlota still lived in Hythe, but had their own establishment at a house called The Dene in Hillside Street.[19]

The Dene, the Hythe home of George and Carlota Mackeson. *Author's collection*

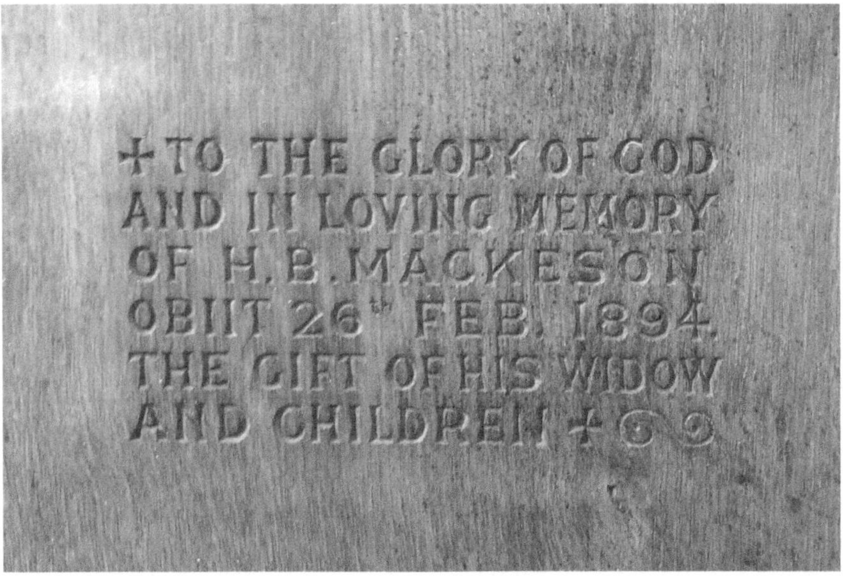

The inscription on the choir pews donated to St Leonard's church.
Author's collection

Mrs Mackeson senior began to reorganise her life. To commemorate her late husband, she and the family presented to St Leonard's church a set of oak choir stalls. She then donated to Folkestone Museum six cases of minerals and fossils, maps and antiquities and later gave the 'bones of a mammoth & co'.[20] Presumably, none of Henry Bean's children wanted these things.

Henry Bean must have been a larger-than-life figure. The number and variety of his interests and commitments outside the brewery make it impossible not to wonder how much time he was able to give to his wife and family, despite the lustre of benevolence that covered everything else he did. The lack of interest they displayed after his death in any of his hobbies and non-business activities is perhaps indicative of a lack of connection with the man.

By the time of her daughter Annie's wedding in 1896 to John le Mestre Hutchison, Mrs Mackeson was living once again in The Elms.[21] The groom was a naval officer and Annie (known as Pansie) joined him at his posting in Cornwall.

George, meanwhile, was indulging his passion for cricket. By 1892, he had taken charge of his father's 'Mr Mackeson's Team' and had recruited to the side one of the brewery's employees who showed particular cricketing talent.[22] He was Charles Kortright, who later played for Essex and whose *Wisden* obituary of 1953 describes him as 'probably the fastest bowler in the history of the game'.[23] Batsmen quite rightly found him terrifying. Kortright also played for Hythe Cricket Club and as a result the Folkestone club was soundly trounced at their encounter in 1892, being dismissed for 23 runs. The next year, playing against the School of Musketry, Kortwight took five wickets with successive balls.[24]

Apparently, Kortright was studying brewing. His wealthy father had insisted that he learn how to make a living. He left the brewery in 1897, but played at Hythe Cricket Week for twenty-one seasons.[25] The sincerity of his brewing ambition may be judged from his entry in the 1939 National Register as 'brewer, retired since 1897'.

Hythe Cricket Week had been instigated by George in his role as secretary of Hythe Cricket Club. The first, in 1894 was a great success. The Venetian Fete – a tableau of decorated floats on the Royal Military Canal – was revived for it and it was estimated that 5,000 visitors came to the town, good news indeed for tradesmen and hoteliers.[26] The cricket club made a profit of £70 and decided to repeat the event.[27]

The next year, Cricket Week was even more successful, though an unplanned event added to the general excitement: the north end of the Ladies' Walk bridge across the canal collapsed, the number of people crowded on it proving too much for its rotting timbers.[28]

Cricket Week became the highlight of every August in Hythe – it ran, with an interruption for the First World War, until 1939. From 1902 residents and visitors could enjoy a varied programme: a parade of decorated bicycles; a torchlight tattoo and a dramatic rescue by firemen from a burning building (a canvas 'house' erected near the cricket pavilion). Local grandees and businesses put up decorated hospitality tents near the cricket pitch, and there was nearly always a fancy dress ball and carnival on the ground, and a concert at Hythe Institute.

Although he was a long-serving member of the Kent County Cricket Club, George had no ambitions to enter public life, and reputedly avoided publicity of any kind.[29] In 1894, he was asked to stand for election as an alderman of Hythe, but declined.[30] He did, however, agree to become a churchwarden at St Leonard's.[31] In his private life, there was sadness. Carlota gave birth to a stillborn daughter in 1893 and a son, also stillborn, in 1899.[32] There would be no more children.

In the five years since their father's death, the Mackeson brothers had worked to modernise the brewery and widen its investment base. Then, almost ninety-nine years to the day after their grandfather and great uncle, Harry and Will Mackeson, had signed the indenture that secured the brewery, Young Henry and George made the biggest change of all.

14

Make Stout More Nourishing

In October 1900, the local newspaper published the prospectus for Mackeson and Co. Ltd, which had been formed to acquire the brewery and maltings. It had, the prospectus stated, a total of sixty-five public houses valued at just over £182,000. The total value of the business was put at £240,505 11*s* 8*d*. The average annual profit was about £16,500. Six thousand preference shares, which attracted a fixed rate of return of 5 per cent, were offered together with a slightly lower number of ordinary shares.

The rest of the cost was to be raised by debenture stock, redeemable after ten years at a rate of 5 per cent. There were two debenture trustees: Myles Fenton, formerly general manager of the South Eastern Railway, and the Mackesons' brother-in-law, Richard Green, who had married their sister Mary Jane.[1] The question of a conflict of interest between Green's two roles seems not to have been raised.

The first shareholders were all family, too: Young Henry and George and their wives; and three of their sisters. The Mackeson brothers were to be the only directors and Stephen Godden the secretary.[2] The very first board meeting took place at the brewery on 26 October 1900, when it was agreed to pay Godden £300 per annum and to give him a month's holiday each year – a very generous offer when working men usually had only bank holidays off (and that only since 1871) and a lucky clerk might be granted a week off in the summer.[3]

Why did they decide to make the family business a limited company? Since 1886, brewers had been allowed to make this change and there were considerable benefits. The new status separated the Mackesons' personal assets and liabilities from those of the business; it gave protection from personal bankruptcy; it made it easier for them to attract investment and finance growth. In the short term, cash would be freed up for the personal use of the Mackeson brothers and there were tax advantages. The Mackesons were not alone: forty-two Kent brewers made the same decision.[4]

One of their early resolutions, in 1903, was that all employees should be members of a benefit society. Otherwise called friendly societies, these were mutual insurance schemes to which men and women paid a weekly premium and would, in case of sickness or unemployment, receive benefits. Until National Insurance was introduced to the UK in 1911, these provided a safety net for working people who might otherwise have faced the workhouse or relied on charity. The Mackesons undertook to pay in full any employee unable to work through ill heath, less the amount received from the society.[5]

There were two friendly societies active in Hythe at this time: the Independent Order of Odd Fellows and the Ancient Order of Foresters. The former seems to have been more popular in the town and had three branches, for men, women and juveniles. It was in the process of building its own large premises in the High Street.

The Mackesons were also generally sympathetic towards the limitations of their older workers. In 1912 the *Folkestone Herald* noted:

> Messrs. Mackeson do not pose as philanthropists, but they keep on their old hands as long as they are able to do the least bit of work; long service is not rewarded with the 'sack' there.[6]

Three years later, reminiscing to a local journalist on the occasion of his golden wedding (a rarity then), Charles Amos recalled his fifty-eight years' employment with the brewery. Although retired, he was still doing odd jobs for the firm, which he praised as a generous employer, especially where 'old hands' were concerned.[7]

The brothers now repeated their ploy of buying a brewery and closing it. In 1907 it was the turn of the Sun Brewery in Littlebourne. The owner, Humphrey de Trafford, had died young and the brewery, together with six public houses, was auctioned. Having no further use for the brewery buildings, the Mackesons had them demolished.

They continued to invest in high-quality equipment for the Hythe site. A visitor to the brewery in 1968, when it was in the process of being demolished, noted approvingly the copper, bought from George Adlam and Sons, brass founders of Bristol, in 1910; a Lancashire boiler dating from 1903 and a Galloway boiler from Gimson and Company of Leicester, 'dating from 1915 and still in use'.[8]

The Mackesons' private lives now were, as far as is known, quiet and mostly unreported and undocumented. In 1905, Young Henry and his wife produced a son after ten years of marriage and the birth of a stillborn daughter. The son, named Harry Ripley, was given an extravagant christening at St Leonard's church: George was his godfather, the brewery employees were allowed time off to attend and were given a party afterwards and a reception for guests was held in Folkestone.[9] Harry Ripley's brother, Graham Lawrie, came into the world two years later.

Old Mrs Mackeson donated eighty of Henry Bean's books to the Hythe Institute library, sold the grand piano and moved to Tonbridge, where her daughter Mary lived. George continued as secretary of the cricket club and in winter played at the local golf club, established in 1894. Life went on.

Then someone at the brewery got interested in the idea of milk beers. Was it Young Henry? Or George? Or a brewery worker? History is silent. It was not an entirely new idea. In 1875, John Henry Johnson had filed a patent for milk beer based on whey, lactose and hops. Lactose, a type of milk sugar, cannot be fermented by brewers' yeast and the residue adds sweetness and body to the finished product. In 1896, John Henry Hooker, manager of the Condensed Peptonised Milk Company, patented another milk beer using a different brewing process. Neither of these were ever manufactured, though the Mackeson brewery did try an unsuccessful test brew in 1907.[10] They were, in fact, then pinning their hopes on another of their bottled beers, Judge Brand, which they were promoting heavily and had registered with its own trademark.

However, in January 1908, William James Melhuish, then working as a lecturer in dietetics, applied to the Patent Office to register his invention, milk stout, a thick, dark stout with very low carbonation. It was accepted in January 1909 and in May, Melhuish assigned his patent rights to the Mackesons. In return, they employed him to act as their consulting analyst, paying him a salary of one third of their net profits on the product.[11]

Milk stout was launched with much publicity. A booklet headlined 'Make Stout More Nourishing' claimed that the beverage gave drinkers 'energy, stopped distension, fulness, indigestion and headache, prevented rheumatism and was ideal for nursing mothers and invalids'. The bottle label announced that 'each pint contains the energising carbohydrates of 10 ounces of pure dairy milk'.[12] The claimed restorative properties of the drink were extravagant and entirely unproven, but the Mackesons, like all brewers, were in competition with a powerful temperance movement and did not have to worry about an Advertising Standards Authority.

Their claims for their beverage were, in fact, quite modest when compared to those of other traders. Wolfe's schnapps was, it was claimed, 'recommended by hundreds of doctors' because 'it is a real health tonic owing to its cleansing action on the liver, kidneys and other organs';[13] Worthington's ale 'builds up the constitution and promotes energy and stamina';[14] and Wincarnis tonic wine, 'revitalises and rejuvenates the vital organs of the body'.[15]

Whatever their veracity, the promotions worked. Mackeson Milk Stout was a huge success and demand soon exceeded the brewery's capacity to supply it. The Mackesons granted licences to other breweries to make and sell the product using their own brand. By 1912 there were fourteen. That year, they also obtained the Australian milk stout patent.[16] Inevitably, some brewers tried to produce milk stout without being licensed. They were quickly dealt with. In 1910, the Mackesons successfully opposed the grant of letters patent to one Ernest Spencer and in 1912 sued R.H. Jenner and Sons for selling beer labelled as milk stout.[17]

The effects of all this activity on the working arrangements at the brewery and on the lives of all concerned must have been huge. The brewery was no longer a modest, small-town concern but a business with national and international connections.

Melhuish continued to experiment with his invention. His original recipe contained pure lactose in powder form, which could be difficult to obtain, so he devised a means of obtaining lactose from sweet whey, a by-product of cheese-making, which was also cheaper.

The future must have looked rosy, but if so, that vision was dashed by international events and the declaration of war on 28 July 1914. Young Henry and George both became special constables and joined the Volunteer Fencibles, a civil defence force. Their wives were involved in caring for the wounded, Ella at Folkestone VAD hospital and Carlota at the Bevan hospital in Sandgate. At first, the brewery was not much affected, though some young employees joined up immediately. The Mackesons had to start advertising for women to work in the bottling department in September 1915, to fill the gaps.[18]

By late 1915 it was clear to Asquith's coalition government that it was not possible to continue fighting the war by relying on voluntary recruits, even though a million men had answered the call. Conscription was necessary and in January 1916 the Military Service Act was passed. All single men aged between 18 and 41 would be called up, except the medically unfit, clergymen, teachers and some industrial workers. In May 1916 conscription was extended to married men. In 1918, the age limit was raised to 51. Military service tribunals were set up for those who thought they should be exempt.

George was at one of the earliest of these, in March 1916, arguing in favour of Charles Heron, a motor driver and mechanic at the brewery. Heron was, he said, indispensable as the brewery had already lost forty-four men. The tribunal disagreed, but deferred Heron's call-up for two months.[19] Heron did not wait for two months, but accepted the inevitable and joined up two weeks later. He served as a private in the Royal Army Service Corps and spent his war at Woolwich Dockyard. The brewery went on to lose four of his successors as drivers to military service.

The next month the brewery was advertising vacancies again and offering to arrange transport from Folkestone if needed.[20] They then re-worded all their situations vacant advertisements to specify that they were only open to those 'not liable for military service'.[21] In June, George was back at the tribunal on behalf of his brewer, Roma Nobile, the analytical chemist successor to Melhuish. By now, George said, he had lost fifty-one men and another twenty-five were of military age. Nobile got a four-month extension, but eventually joined the Royal Army Medical Corps.[22]

By 1917, the brewery was struggling. Ninety of their men were now serving their country and the Mackesons could barely fulfil their contracts with the government to supply the military camps that encircled Hythe, accommodating men waiting to go to France. These had to some extent compensated for the loss of income generated by the restrictions placed on licensing hours from 1914. In Folkestone, public houses now shut at 8 p.m.[23] All the brewery's clerical staff, bar the supervisor, were new and inexperienced. The erstwhile company secretary Herbert Cole, who had succeeded Stephen Godden, was now a sergeant major in Aldershot. In an unprecedented move, the brewery even advertised for women to drive their horse vans.[24]

In May that year, Hythe experienced at first hand the horrors of modern warfare. Gotha bombers, aiming for London, turned back because of low cloud and passed over Kent. Sixteen planes, flying abreast, approached the town. The air-raid warning – a black flag flown from the church tower – was not showing. Several bombs were dropped on Hythe. Three failed to explode, but two dropped through houses in Cobden Road and West Parade. Seven fell on the beach and in gardens and allotments; one fell on the golf course and another exploded above the Metropole Steam Laundry. The verger, Daniel Lyth was mortally injured by shrapnel in the churchyard, and Amy Turner of Ormonde Road, who had stepped outside to call her children in, was also killed. The last two bombs fell on rough ground and the Imperial Hotel golf course.

The Gothas flew on to Shorncliffe, killing eighteen military personnel, and then to Folkestone. A single bomb was dropped on Tontine Street, killing sixty-nine people, mostly women and children queuing outside a greengrocery. The Mackesons' Brewery Tap sustained damage to its roof and windows; the wine and spirit shop they had opened a few doors along the street had its windows blown out and the stock destroyed, but no one was hurt in either establishment.

After the raid, serious thought was given in Hythe to air-raid precautions and in December, after giant Zeppelin-Staaken bombers were seen over the town, the Mackeson brothers offered to empty their brewery cellars to provide an air-raid shelter for up to 1,000 people.[25] They were ready for use by January 1918 (although the Town Council took the government's advice not to sound air-raid sirens: it was believed that these would cause panic and make people run out into the street, whereas they would be safer indoors).

Not all the brewery's servicemen came home. The names of six Hythe men who worked for the Mackesons appear on the town's war memorial: Joseph Channon; Ernest Rogers, drayman; Percy Smith, labourer; George Stokes, bottle washer; Walter Tugwell, bottler; and Stephen Vidler, bottle washer.

It seemed in 1919 as though a new start could be made and the Mackesons invested in state-of-the art equipment: a 'continuous combined beer chiller and carbonator' for £700, a condenser for nearly £1,000 and a Pontiflex twenty-eight-head bottling machine for £310.[26]

The traditional way of producing bottled beers was to put a little sugar and yeast into each bottle. The bottles would then be kept at a stable temperature for a few days so that the yeast metabolised the sugar into more alcohol and carbon dioxide, which naturally carbonated the beer. Often publicans would need to store the bottles themselves for this carbonation to take place and they always needed an additional storage time for the yeast to settle after transportation. The beer was then carefully decanted into glasses, leaving the yeast sediment behind.

If the crate of bottles was accidentally disturbed, it would need settling again, hence another delay.

The new system took filtered, chilled beer and then artificially carbonated it. Cold beer can absorb a lot more carbon dioxide, enabling the bottle to be filled and capped before all of the gas has a chance to escape. Apart from being fully carbonated on arrival, the bottles could be manhandled as there was no sediment to disturb. Publicans much preferred the new system as the beer was delivered ready to drink and was easier to pour.

In May 1920, Hythe woke to stunning news. On 10 May, Young Henry and George held their usual board meeting. The next day, they transferred their shares in the company to five members of the Simonds brewing company and resigned as directors. The Hythe brewery was now owned by Messrs. H. and G. Simonds, brewers of Bridge Street, Reading. There was no name change – the brand was too well known – and operations continued in Hythe as before.

The war years had been tough and had seen annual profits slump to just £10,600.[27] Young Henry was now 59 and George 55, and probably both were thinking of retirement. Perhaps they did not want to die 'in harness', as their father and grandfather had done. Their mother, who would have remembered the brewery from as long ago as the 1860s, had died in 1919. Young Henry's sons, now in their teens, were both destined for the army. But Mackeson Milk Stout was undoubtedly a huge success and now the war was over, profits began to rise again. By the time of the sale, they were at £15,148 and the firm was paying its shareholders dividends of 10 per cent.[28]

The Mackeson brothers had no idea how long this expansion would last. Perhaps they felt it was better to sell a successful concern rather than wait for the downturn in the market for milk stout, or maybe they just lacked the interest and energy to continue marketing and promoting a best-selling product. They were also part of a process of consolidation of breweries that was taking place. By the end of the 1920s, all the indigenous Kent breweries, except Shepherd Neame, had been taken over by outsiders.[29]

It was quite usual also at this time to see successful businessmen, in late middle age, make a move away from active business towards rentier income as it was also the norm to see their sons move towards the professions rather than the family trade.[30]

Young Henry and his wife had already moved to Littlebourne, near Canterbury, then a rural village with a population of fewer than 1,000. They had achieved respectability in Folkestone, but respectability was not gentility. However, their impetus towards it continued. Their sons were at Rugby School, not just being educated but making connections for the future. Young Henry's sisters had all married well, thus fulfilling the purpose of their education and also creating more connections in polite society. In the countryside, he and Ella could narrow the gap between themselves and the county gentry. Young Henry showed a belated interest in public life by acting as a magistrate and got involved in country life by becoming a senior judge of barley at the Royal Agricultural Hall. Ella joined the Women's Institute and the Mothers' Union. Their separation from the brewery seemed complete.

Ella died in 1933. Her obituary noted:

> Mrs Mackeson was a daughter of Mr Holdsworth Ripley, a well-known member of the London Stock Exchange, and of Mrs Holdworth Ripley. Her two brothers, Messrs. Albert and Snip Ripley were famous amateur steeplechase jockeys. She was married in 1895 to Mr Henry Mackeson, son of Mr Henry Bean Mackeson of Hythe, where the family have owned extensive property for over a hundred years.[31]

The brewery gets a passing mention towards the end, but Ella's pedigree and the Mackesons' land holdings were clearly the vital components of the biography.

Young Henry died in 1935. He and Ella are buried together in St Leonard's churchyard.

George stayed in Hythe, at The Dene. In 1936, he and Edward Osborne, businessman and former mayor of Hythe, paid for a new organ to be installed in St Leonard's church. It was dedicated by the

Archbishop of Canterbury in May that year. George died at home on 28 January 1950. He had continued for many years as church warden and, until his death, as president of Hythe Cricket Club. When he died, he left the cricket ground, which he owned, to his nephews, with the stipulation it should always be used for cricket. The family eventually sold it to the club in 1993 and cricket is played there still.

The grave stone of Young Henry and Ella Mackeson in St Leonard's churchyard, Hythe. *Author's collection*

15

By Golly It Does You Good

There was still to be one last link between the Mackesons and Hythe. Harry Ripley, after an education at Rugby School and Sandhurst College, was commissioned in the Royal Scots Greys, an elite and ancient cavalry regiment. He was promoted captain in 1936 and lieutenant colonel in 1940. After D-Day he commanded an armoured brigade and was involved in heavy fighting in the advance from Normandy to Ghent. By the end of the Second World War, he was a brigadier. He had married Alethea Cecil Chetwynd-Talbot, daughter of Reginald George Chetwynd-Talbot, on 22 February 1940. The Duchess of Gloucester, one of the bride's cousins, was at the wedding.

As the war was drawing to a close, Harry Ripley's uncle George Mackeson was re-elected as president of the Hythe Conservative Association. Weeks later, the town's MP, Commander Rupert Brabner, a much-decorated Royal Navy pilot, was killed when the plane taking him to Canada was lost over the Azores. In May 1945, Harry Ripley was chosen by the Hythe Conservatives as their prospective parliamentary candidate. He beat two others to the post: Colonel David Jackling, who had also been born in Hythe (the son of a bank manager) and was serving with the Coldstream Guards, and Captain Russell, nominated by Conservative Central Office. Harry Ripley had already been selected by Horncastle Conservative Association, but withdrew in April, citing his doctor's opinion that his heath was to poor for him to take on such a large constituency.[1]

In Kent, however, it was reported that he and Alethea simply wanted to live in the neighbourhood of Hythe.[2]

The local press approved of Harry Ripley. He was, they said, 'hefty in build, has a voice like a Sergt.-Major of the Guards and a direct, forthright manner. He is definitely not a Yes-man.' He also, they reported, had a very good understanding of local issues.[3]

Hythe had voted Conservative since 1895, and Brabner had secured a comfortable majority in 1939. Harry Ripley had other advantages: the brewery bearing his name still stood in the town; his family were well known and he and his wife had impeccable war records – Alethea had joined the Auxiliary Territorial Service as a private. The Labour candidate was only 21 and from Hertfordshire; the Liberal man was from Teignmouth.

Harry Ripley threw himself into electioneering, attending VE teas, whist drives and memorial services, visiting women workers at the Metropole steam laundry and talking to fishermen, often accompanied by Uncle George. On election day, the Conservative Party 'flooded the streets with cars'.[4] All this, though, produced a final majority of less than 2,000, in a country that had turned its back on Winston Churchill and the Tories and voted in a Labour government.

The constituency of Hythe was abolished in 1950 and became part of the new Folkestone and Hythe constituency. Harry stood again in the general election that year, on a patriotic and anti-nationalisation ticket. He wanted, he wrote, to 'preserve what is best in the British Way of Life', and to reinforce the point, his election jeep was festooned with red, white and blue bunting.[5] It worked. His majority was now nearly 10,000 and to celebrate he blew the ancient moot horn at Hythe town hall. In the snap general election of 1951, his majority was even larger.

Harry Ripley served under Winston Churchill as Deputy Chief Whip, as a Lord of the Treasury and as Secretary for Overseas Trade. In the 1954 New Year's Honours list he was created a baronet for public and political services and chose the title 'of Hythe in the County of Kent'. In the 1955 election he was once again returned with a comfortable majority. He did not seek re-election in 1959, saying he wanted more time for his family and business interests, and he retired to Great Mongeham. The family had come full circle. The village was the birthplace of his great-great-grandmother Elizabeth Bean and the burial place of the first Henry Mackeson.

Sir Harry Ripley Mackeson died in January 1964 aged 58 and was succeeded in the baronetcy by his son Rupert.

In 1929, Simonds sold the Mackeson brewery to Jude, Hanbury & Co., which in turn came under the control of Whitbread. At first the new owners doubted whether it was worth continuing to brew the product. They tweaked the recipe and ran a publicity campaign. Milk stout had a new lease of life. A 1936 leaflet spoke of its popularity 'from Cornwall to Caithness'.

A shortage of whey during the Second World War led to the removal of the word 'milk' from the stout's labels and a 1946 decree from the Ministry of Food forbade mention of the word in the brewery's advertising. This did not stop the beer's continuing success and nearly half a million barrels a year were still being produced in 1961. As part of the publicity, Colonel Whitbread established the Mackeson Gold Cup, run at Cheltenham, in 1960 (though it has since become the Paddy Power Gold Cup). The character actor Bernard Miles was recruited for TV advertisements in which he declaimed, in a broad Mummerset brogue, that Mackeson Stout 'Looks good, tastes good and by golly it does you good'. The notion that it was a 'healthy' drink and suitable for women persisted. Well into the 1970s, nursing mothers in NHS hospitals were offered a nightly glass of 'Mackies'. And in the Rovers' Return, Ena Sharples, Minnie Caldwell and Martha Longhurst enjoyed many a tipple of milk stout.

Whitbread shut the Hythe brewery in 1968, citing the economic climate of the time, and made fifty men and women redundant. Milk stout was brewed elsewhere. It found favour in places a long way from the fictional Weatherfield, was exported to over sixty countries and brewed under licence in Belgium, New Zealand, Jamaica, Singapore and Trinidad, where a stronger version was marketed as 'King of the Night'. Today it is still available in the UK from some supermarkets in cans.

The demolition of the Mackesons' Hythe brewery. *Author's collection*

Supermarkets and cans would be mysterious concepts to Harry and Will Mackeson, as would so much else in the twenty-first century. The Hythe they knew has all but disappeared under the unstoppable march of modernisation. The brewery was demolished and the site is now occupied by sheltered housing. Only the original malthouse and The Elms remain. But scattered across Hythe there are other reminders of the Mackesons' long presence in the town. The sheltered housing development, Mackeson Court; Henry Bean's name on the gilded list of mayors in the town hall; the vault built into the side of St Leonard's church; the graves outside; the choir pews and the organ inside the church bearing the Mackeson name; Mackeson Square near the brewery site; and the Mackeson breweriana in the town museum. A cursory internet search of 'Mackeson' today will throw up multiple references to the family's most famous product, but for the town of Hythe they were so much more than just milk stout.

BIBLIOGRAPHY

Allen, Charles, *Soldier Sahibs: The Men Who Made the North-West Frontier* (London: John Murray, 2000).

Bell, Florence, *At the Works: A Study of a Manufacturing Town* (London: Arnold, 1907).

Boorman, David, *Hythe Cricket Week, 1894–1939* (Horsham: 2016).

Bulley, Anne, *Bombay Country Ships 1790–1833* (London: British Library, 1995).

Cobbett, William, *Rural Rides* (London: Penguin Classics, 2001).

Corran, H.S., *A History of Brewing* (Newton Abbot: David and Charles, 1975).

Dalrymple, William, *The Anarchy: The Relentless Rise of the East India Company* (London: Bloomsbury, 2019).

—*White Mughals: Love and Betrayal in Eighteenth-Century India* (London: Bloomsbury, 2002).

Davidoff, Leonore, *Family Fortunes: Men and Women of the English Middle Class, 1780–1850* (London: Hutchinson, 1987).

Digby, Anne, *Making a Medical Living: Doctors and Patients in the English Market for Medicine, 1720–1911* (Cambridge: Cambridge University Press, 1994).

D'Oyly, Charles, *Tom Raw: A Burlesque Poem in Twelve Cantos: Illustrated by Twenty-Five Engravings, Descriptive of a Cadet in the East India Company* (London: Rudolph Ackermann, 1828).

Dyhouse, Carol, *Girls Growing up in Late Victorian and Edwardian England* (London: Routledge, 1981).

Easdown, Martin and Thomas Genth, *A Glint in the Sky: German Air Attacks on Folkestone, Dover, Ramsgate, Margate* (London: Leo Cooper, 2004).

Farringdon, Anthony, *A Biographical Index of East India Company Maritime Service Officers, 1600–1834* (London: British Library, 1999).

—*A Catalogue of East India Company Ships' Journals and Logs 1604–1834* (London: British Library, 1999).

Filmer, Richard, *Hops and Hop Picking* (Risborough: Shire Publications, 1998).

Floud, Roger, and Donald McCloskey, *The Economic History of Britain since 1700, Vol. 1 1700–1860* (Cambridge: Cambridge University Press, 1994).

Forbes, Duncan, *Hythe Haven: The Story of the Town and Cinque Port of Hythe* (Hythe: Shearwater Press, 1982).

Foster, Terry, *Brewing Porters and Stouts* (New York: Skyhorse Publishing, 2014).

Fraser, Derek, *The Evolution of the British Welfare State: A History of Social Policy Since the Industrial Revolution* (London: MacMillan, 1973).

Gardner, Brian, *The East India Company: A History* (Dorchester: Dorset Press, 1990).

George, Michael and Martin George, *Coast of Conflict: The Story of the South Kent Coast* (Seaford: S.B. Publications, 2004).

Glover, Steve, and Michael Rogers, *The Old Pubs of Deal and Walmer with Kingsdown and Mongeham* (Whitstable: Bygone Publishing, 2010).

Gray, Adrian, *South Eastern Railway* (Haslemere: Middleton Press, 1990).

Hackman, Rowan, *Ships of the East India Company* (Gravesend: World Ship Society, 2001).

Hart, Brian, *The Hythe and Sandgate Railway* (Didcot: Wild Swan Publications, 1987).

Hobsbawm, Eric, *Industry and Empire from 1750 to the Present Day* (London: Wiedenfeld and Nicolson, 1968).

Hollingsworth, J.P., *And Then There Was Beer: The Story of Kentish Breweries* (Ayrshire: Stenlake Publishing, 2016).

Jasanoff, Maya, *Edge of Empire: Lives, Culture and Conquest in the East, 1750–1850* (New York: Alfred A. Knopf, 2005).

Lawson, Terence, and David Killingray, *An Historical Atlas of Kent* (Andover: Phillimore, 2004).

Longford, Elizabeth, *Queen Victoria* (London: Wiedenfeld and Nicolson, 1964)

McGonigal, Christopher, *The Deedes Family in Hythe Kent, 1580–1800* (Hythe: Hythe Civic Society, 2021).

Mackeson, Henry Bean, *The Fraternity of the Assumption of the Blessed Virgin Mary at Hythe* (London: John Russell Smith, 1863).

Malchow, H.L., *Gentleman Capitalists: The Social and Political World of the Victorian Businessman* (Stanford: Stanford University Press, 1992).

Mathias, Peter, *The Brewing Industry in England, 1700–1830* (Cambridge: Cambridge University Press, 1959).

Monkton, H.A., *A History of English Ale and Beer* (London: Bodley Head, 1966).

Peaty, Ian P., *You Brew Good Ale: A History of Small Scale Brewing* (Stroud: Sutton, 1997).

Peters, Douglas M., 'Between Mars and Mammon; The East India Company and Efforts to Reform Its Army, 1796–1832', *The Historical Journal*, Vol. 33, No. 2, pp.385–401.

Philips, C.H., *The East India Company, 1784–1834* (Manchester: Manchester University Press, 1961).

Phillips, Nicola, *Women in Business, 1700–*1850 (Suffolk: The Boydell Press, 2006).

Pietsch, Roland, *The Real Jim Hawkins: Ships' Boys in the Georgian Navy* (Barnsley: Seaforth Publishing, 2011).

Porter, Roy, *The Greatest Benefit to Mankind: A Medical History of Humanity from Antiquity to the Present* (London: HarperCollins, 1997).

Preston, James, *Malting and Malthouses in Kent* (Stroud: Amberley Publishing, 2015).

Richardson, Nigel, *Thring of Uppingham, Victorian Educator* (Buckingham: University of Buckingham Press, 2014).

Richmond, Lesley and Alison Turtle (eds.), *The Brewing Industry: A Guide to Historical Records* (Manchester: Manchester University Press, 1990).

Scull, Andrew T., *Museums of Madness: The Social Organisation of Insanity in Nineteenth Century England* (London: Allen Lane, 1979).

Sramek, Joseph, *Gender, Morality and Race in Company India, 1765–1858* (London: Palgrave MacMillan, 2011).
Steinbach, Susie, *Women in England 1760–1914: A Social History* (London: Wiedenfeld & Nicholson, 2005).
Tames, Richard, *The Victorian Public House* (Princes Risborough: Shire Publications, 2003).
Westly, F., *A guide to Young Brewers: particularly adapted to the families of the nobility and gentry, farmers and private brewers, by a practical brewer* (1820).
Williamson, Thomas, *The East India Vade-Mecum, or Complete Guide for Gentlemen Intended for the Civil, Military or Naval Service of the Hon. East India Company* (London: Black, Parry and Kingsbury, 1810).
Wilson, Adrian, *The Making of Man-Midwifery: Childbirth in England 1660–1770* (London: UCL Press, 1995).

NOTES

Note on References

BL	The British Library
KHLC	Kent History and Library Centre
NA	The National Archives

Prologue

1 Roger Floud and Donald McCloskey, *The Economic History of Britain since 1700, Vol. 1 1700–1860* (Cambridge: Cambridge University Press, 1994), p.391.
2 KHLC: H1395. Evacuation Schedule.
3 KHLC: Hy/T3/8.
4 F.H. Fanton, 'Turnpike Roads in the Canterbury Area', *Archaeologia Cantiana*, Vol. 138, 2017, pp.171–91.
5 *Kentish Gazette*, 24 July 1801.
6 *Kentish Gazette*, 6 February 1798.

Chapter 1

1 KHLC: EK/U47/34/T12.
2 KHLC: U47/34/1.
3 Steve Glover and Michael Rogers, *The Old Pubs of Deal and Walmer with Kingsdown and Mongeham* (Whitstable: Bygone Publishing, 2010).
4 KHLC: EK/ U11/C4.
5 NA: IR series 64 f 197, accessed via www.findmypast.co.uk
6 *Kentish Gazette*, 30 July 1793.
7 John Leake, *A Lecture Introductory to the Theory and Practice of Midwifery* (1792), quoted in Anne Digby, *Making a Medical Living: Doctors and Patients in the English Market for Medicine, 1720–1911* (Cambridge: Cambridge University Press, 1994).
8 *Kentish Weekly Post*, 12 December 1800.

9 KHLC: EK/U511 E2-3.
10 KHLC: EK/U511/A8.
11 KHLC: EK/U511/C51/2/2.
12 *Ibid.*
13 Glover and Rogers.
14 KHLC: NR/JW209.
15 *Kentish Weekly Post or Canterbury Journal*, 24 December 1802.
16 NA: PROB 11/1372/32.
17 KHLC: H1395.
18 KHLC: EK/U47/34/T11.
19 KHLC: EK/U511/C8.
20 KHLC: EK/U3555/4/M/Bp/1/1.
21 KHLC: EK/U3555/4/M/Bf2/3/3.
22 KHLC: NR/JW/209.
23 KHLC: EK/U3555/4/M/Bf2/3/1.
24 *Ibid.*
25 Nick Redman in *What's Brewing*, March 1995, pp.6–7.
26 Peter Mathias, *The Brewing Industry in England 1700–1830* (Cambridge: Cambridge University Press, 1959), p.25.
27 Richard Tames, *The Victorian Public House* (Princes Risborough, Shire Publications, 2003), p.8.
28 KHLC: EK/U511/E6.
29 KHLC: EK/U47/34/T12.
30 KHLC: EK/U511/C6.
31 *Ibid.*
32 KHLC: EK/U47/34/B2.
33 KHLC: EK/U47/34/5 and EK/U47/34/6.
34 *Kentish Weekly Post*, 13 September 1803.
35 KHLC EK/U47/34/T18.
36 Frederick S. Peirce, *Dover, Folkestone, Sandgate and Hythe District Directory and Court Guide 1875* (Sinnock, Howard & Co.) and 1881 Census, Hythe, accessed via www.findmypast.co.uk

Chapter 2

1 BL: East India Directory and Register 1797.
2 Maya Jasanoff, *Edge of Empire: Lives, Culture and Conquest in the East, 1750–1850* (New York: Alfred A. Knopf, 2005), p.82.
3 Charles D'Oyly, *Tom Raw: A Burlesque Poem in Twelve Cantos: Illustrated by Twenty-Five Engravings, Descriptive of a Cadet in the East India Company* (London: Rudolph Ackermann, 1828), lines 5441–444.
4 KHLC: EK/U511/E6.
5 BL: East India Directory and Register 1804 and 1805.
6 KHLC: EK/U511/C8.

7 KHLC: EK/U511/E4.
8 Alan Furness, 'The Jamaican coffee boom and John Mackeson: a Blue Mountain coffee plantation 1807–1819', *Jamaican Historical Review*, Vol. III, March 1962, pp.10–21.
9 KHLC: EK/U511/C8.
10 *Ibid.*
11 Quoted in Frank Wesley Pitman, 'Slavery on British West Indies Plantations in the Eighteenth Century', *Journal of Negro History*, Vol. 11, Issue 4, October 1926.
12 KHLC: EK/U511/C8.
13 Jane Austen, *Northanger Abbey* (London: Wordsworth Classics, 1993), p.17.
14 KHLC: EK/U511/C8.
15 *Ibid.*
16 *Ibid.*
17 *Devizes and Wiltshire Gazette*, 18 March 1830.
18 *Morning Post*, 17 December 1790, and *Naval & Military Gazette and Weekly Chronicle*, 23 August 1834.
19 Joseph Foster, *Men-at-the-bar: a biographical hand-list of the members of the various Inns of Court, including Her Majesty's Judges, etc.* 2nd ed. (London and Aylesbury: Hazell, Watson and Viney, Limited, 1885), p.69.
20 *Legacies of British Slavery*, accessed at www.ucl.ac.uk
21 *Wilts and Gloucestershire Standard*, 5 September 1843.

Chapter 3

1 Anthony Farringdon, *A Biographical Index of East India Company Maritime Service Officers, 1600–1834* (London: British Library, 1999).
2 Anthony Farringdon, *Catalogue of East India Company Ships Journals and Logs, 1604–1834* (London: British Library 1999).
3 KHLC: EK/U511/51/2/1.
4 *Ibid.* and & Farringdon.
5 Rowan Hackman, *Ships of the East India Company* (Gravesend, Kent: World Ship Society, 2001).
6 *Madras Courier*, 20 December 1809.
7 *Government Gazette (India)*, 29 March 1810.
8 KHLC: EK/U511/C6.
9 *Ibid.*

Chapter 4

1 KHLC: EK/U47/34/T11.
2 KHLC: EK/U511/C20/1.
3 *Ibid.*
4 *Ibid.*
5 KHLC: EK/U511/C20/1.
6 KHLC: EK/U511/C23/2.
7 KHLC: EK/U511/C20/1.

Chapter 5

1 *Kentish Weekly Post*, 2 April 1805.
2 KHLC: EK/U511/C18.
3 KHLC: EK/U511/C7/1.
4 *Ibid*.
5 KHLC: EK/U511/14/2.
6 KHLC: EK/U511/C23/2.
7 *Sun* (London), 23 March 1829.
8 KHLC: EK/U511/A9 and EK/U511/C20/2.
9 *Kentish Weekly Post*, 27 December 1831.
10 *Kentish Weekly Post*, 15 January 1833.
11 KHLC: EK/U511/C13/1.
12 *Kentish Weekly Post*, 13 October 1833.
13 KHLC: EK/U511/C13/1.
14 KHLC: EK/U511/C28/2.

Chapter 6

1 Records of King's School, Canterbury 1809.
2 KHLC: EK/U511/A11.
3 KHLC: EK/U511/A10.
4 KHLC: EK/U511/C29
5 KHLC: EK/U511/A10.
6 BL: L/MIL/9.114.
7 KHLC: EK/U511/C29.
8 Thomas Williamson, *The East India Vade-Mecum, or Complete Guide for Gentlemen Intended for the Civil, Military or Naval Service of the Hon. East India Company* (London: Black, Parry and Kingsbury, 1810), p.21.
9 *Morning Chronicle*, 9 July 1805.
10 BL: East India Directory and Register 1806, 1807 and 1811.
11 KHLC: EK/U511/C20/1.
12 NA: PROB 11/1706/227.
13 *Bombay Gazette*, 24 March 1819.
14 Without an English education, they could not qualify as Company servants. Cornwallis did not want to create a settled colonial class in India as had happened in America. See William Dalrymple, *White Mughals: Love and Betrayal in Eighteenth-Century India* (London: Bloomsbury, 2002), p.50.
15 Williamson, p.441.
16 General Benoit de Boigne, quoted in Dalrymple, *White Mughals*, p.119.
17 Williamson, p.460.
18 KHLC: EK/U511/C6.
19 KHLC: EK/U511/C7/1.
20 KHLC: EK/U511/C6.
21 *Bombay Gazette*, 25 October 1837 & 1 November 1838.
22 Anne Bulley, *Bombay Country Ships* 1790–1833 (London: British Library, 1995).

23 Parish Register Transcripts from the Presidency of Madras 1698–1948, N-2.17, p.14, accessed via www.familysearch.org
24 *Naval & Military Gazette and Weekly Chronicle of the United Service*, 27 June 1835.
25 Parish register transcripts from the Presidency of Bombay, 1709–1948, N-3-12, p.24, accessed via www.familysearch.org
26 *Ibid.*, p.41.
27 *London Gazette*, 2 May 1837.

Chapter 7

1 KHLC: H1216.
2 KHLC: EK/U511/C33.
3 Redman, pp.6–7.
4 F. Westly, *A guide to Young Brewers: particularly adapted to the families of the nobility and gentry, farmers and private brewers, by a practical brewer* (1820), p.46.
5 KHLC: EK/U511/A13.
6 KHLC: EK/U511/C6.
7 *Kentish Weekly Post*, 24 July 1807.
8 Duncan Forbes, *Hythe Haven, The Story of the Town and Cinque Port of Hythe* (Hythe: Shearwater Press, 1982), p.118.
9 KHLC: U3555/4/M/Bf2/3/1.
10 *Kentish Gazette*, 24 July 1773.
11 Redman, pp.6–7.
12 William Cobbett, *Rural Rides* (London: Penguin Classics, 2001), p.149.

Chapter 8

1 KHLC: EK/U511/B1.
2 KHLC: EK/U511/C6.
3 KHLC: EK/U511/E3.
4 KHLC: EK/U511/C20/1.
5 Admission Records of the King's School, Canterbury.
6 KHLC: U555/4/M/Bp1/1.
7 KHLC: U/511/B1. William Hammond was the Mackesons' banker and Will's co-executor. The nature of his sacrifice is likely to have been in waiving fees and/or interest due on loans.
8 KHLC: EK/U511/C20/1.
9 *Ibid.*
10 KHLC: EK/ U3555/4/M/Bf2/3/1.
11 H.L. Malchow, *Gentleman Capitalists: The Social and Political World of the Victorian Businessman* (Stanford: Stanford University Press, 1992), p.345.
12 *Ibid.*
13 KHLC: EK/U511/C13/1.

14 KHLC: EK/U511/C30.
15 Redman, pp.6–7.
16 *Kentish Weekly Post or Canterbury Journal*, 28 September 1830.
17 *Ibid.*
18 KHLC: EK/U511/C27/2.
19 KHLC: EK/U511/C20/1.
20 *Morning Post*, 7 May 1830.
21 Roland Pietsch, *The Real Jim Hawkins: Ships' Boys in the Georgian Navy* (Barnsley: Seaforth Publishing, 2011).
22 J.A. Richardson, 'A Visit to Haslar', *Journal of the Royal Naval Medical Service*, Vol. 2, 1916, pp.329–339.
23 Quoted in Andrew T. Scull, *Museums of Madness: The Social Organization of Insanity in Nineteenth Century England* (London: Allen Lane, 1979), p.64.
24 *Morning Post*, 9 November 1837.
25 KHLC: U511/C20/1.
26 KHLC: H1217.
27 *Kentish Gazette*, 5 January 1836.

Chapter 9

1 KHLC: EK/U511/C20/1.
2 *Education enquiry: Abstract of the answers and returns made pursuant to an address of the House of Commons, dated 24 May 1833. England and Wales* (London: Home Office, 1835).
3 *Ibid.*
4 *Morning Herald* (London), 15 October 1845.
5 KHLC: EK/U511/C19.
6 KHLC: EK/U511/C24/1.
7 *Ibid.*
8 KHLC: EK/U511/C29.
9 *Dover Telegraph and Cinque Ports General Advertiser*, 16 April 1836.
10 *Canterbury Journal, Kentish Times and Farmers' Gazette*, 12 October 1840.
11 *Kentish Mercury*, 2 May 1840.
12 *Dover Telegraph and Cinque Ports General Advertiser*, 18 January 1834.
13 KHLC: EK/U511/T51/1.
14 KHLC: EK/U511/C24/3.
15 KHLC: U3555/4/M/Bf2/1/1.
16 KHLC: EK/U511 E2-3.
17 Elizabeth Longford, *Queen Victoria* (London: Wiedenfeld and Nicolson, 1964), p.304.
18 Charles Allen, *Soldier Sahibs: The Men Who Made the North-West Frontier* (London: John Murray, 2000), p.225.
19 *Ibid.*, p.226.

20 *Ibid.*, p.76.
21 *South Eastern Gazette*, 20 March 1860.
22 *Folkestone Chronicle*, 31 March 1860.
23 Arthur Hugh Clough, *Say not the struggle nought availeth*, 1847.

Chapter 10

1 *The Globe*, 13 September 1836.
2 *Kentish Weekly Post or Canterbury Journal*, 3 October 1837.
3 *Dover Telegraph*, 7 April 1860.
4 *Kentish Gazette*, 20 November 1860.
5 *Dover Chronicle*, 23 February 1861.
6 *Volunteer Service Gazette and Military Dispatch*, 19 May 1866.
7 *Dover Chronicle*, 19 July 1862.
8 H.B. Mackeson, *The Fraternity of the Assumption of the Blessed Virgin Mary at Hythe* (London: J.R. Smith, 1873).
9 Brian Hart, *The Hythe and Sandgate Railway* (Didcot: Wild Swan Publications, 1987), p.9.
10 *Folkestone Chronicle*, 14 September 1872.
11 Adrian Gray, *South Eastern Railway* (Haslemere: Middleton Press, 1990), p.115.
12 Denise Rayner, unpublished ms, Hythe Civic Society.
13 *Maidstone Journal and Kentish Advertiser*, 23 July 1866.
14 *Kentish Gazette*, 5 December 1865.
15 *South Eastern Gazette*, 29 March 1869.
16 *Kentish Gazette*, 6 April 1869.
17 KHLC: EK/ U3555/4/M/Bf2/1/2.
18 *Dover Telegraph*, 7 January 1863.
19 KHLC: U3555/4/M/Bf2/1/2.
20 *Ibid.*
21 *Ibid.*
22 KHLC: U3555/4/M/Bp5/7.
23 *Ibid.*
24 KHLC: EK/U3555/4/M/Bp/1/1.
25 *Army and Navy Gazette*, 5 January 1867.
26 *Western Morning News*, 2 May 1865.
27 *Army and Navy Gazette*, 11 January 1868.
28 *Kentish Gazette*, 20 February 1866.
29 KHLC: U555/4/M/BP1/1.

Chapter 11

1 Nigel Richardson, *Thring of Uppingham, Victorian Educator*, (Buckingham: University of Buckingham Press, 2014).
2 *Ibid.*, p.168.
3 Quoted in Carol Dyhouse, *Girls Growing up in Late Victorian and Edwardian England* (London: Routledge, 1981), p.42.

4 *Ibid.*
5 KHLC: U3555/4/M/Bf2/1/2.
6 PRO June 1861.
7 *Ardrossan and Saltcoats Herald*, 23 February 1878.
8 KHLC: UK/U3555/4/M/Bp/1/1, Will of H.B. Mackeson.
9 *Folkestone Express, Sandgate, Shorncliffe & Hythe Advertiser*, 20 October 1894.
10 *Maidstone Journal*, 24 November 1866.

Chapter 12

1 KHLC: EK/U3555/4/M/Bf2/1/2.
2 1891 Census, Hythe, accessed via www.findmypast.co.uk
3 KHLC: EK/U3555/4/M/Bf2/1/2.
4 *Folkestone, Hythe, Sandgate & Cheriton Herald*, 13 September 1930.
5 *Whitstable Times and Herne Bay Herald*, 3 April 1875.
6 *Kentish Gazette*, 31 May 1887, and *South Wales Echo*, 2 June 1887.
7 KHLC: EK/2008/2/92 (11).
8 KHLC: EK/2008/2/128 (1-6).
9 *Folkestone Express, Sandgate, Shorncliffe & Hythe Advertiser*, 8 October 1887.
10 KHLC: EK/U3555/4/M/Bf2/1/1.
11 James Preston, *Malting and Malthouses in Kent* (Stroud: Amberley Publishing, 2015), p.28.
12 *Folkestone Express, Sandgate, Shorncliffe & Hythe Advertiser*, 4 November 1876.
13 *Ibid.*, 4 August 1877.
14 *Eastbourne Gazette*, 16 June 1880.
15 *East Kent Gazette*, 24 April 1886.
16 *Kentish Gazette*, 29 May 1886.
17 KHLC: EK/U3555/4/M/Bf2/1/2.
18 KHLC: EK/U3555/4/M/Bf2/3/4.
19 *Kentish Gazette*, 17 December 1887.
20 *Folkestone Express, Sandgate, Shorncliffe & Hythe Advertiser*, 22 June 1880.
21 *Folkestone Express, Sandgate, Shorncliffe & Hythe Advertiser*, 9 July 1884.
22 *Kent Times*, 10 March 1888.
23 *Canterbury Journal, Kentish Times and Farmers' Gazette*, 28 April 1888.
24 *Folkestone, Hythe, Sandgate & Cheriton Herald*, 17 September 1932.
25 KHLC: H/U21/F6.
26 *Folkestone Express, Sandgate, Shorncliffe & Hythe Advertiser*, 7 March 1894.
27 KHLC: U555/4/M/Bp1/1.

Chapter 13

1 KHLC: EK/U3555/4/M/Bp/1/10.
2 *Folkestone Express, Sandgate, Shorncliffe & Hythe Advertiser*, 22 March 1899.
3 *Ibid.*, 22 May 1897.
4 *Dover Express*, 18 August 1899.
5 KHLC: U3555/4/M/Bf2/3/4.

6 Preston, p.97.
7 'Reflections of a Brewery Foreman', *The House of Whitbread Journal*, October 1936.
8 *Folkestone Express, Sandgate, Shorncliffe & Hythe Advertiser*, 18 March 1899.
9 *Ibid.*, 1 July 1891.
10 *Folkestone Chronicle*, 30 January 1892.
11 *Deal, Walmer & Sandwich Mercury*, 25 March 1893.
12 *Folkestone Express, Sandgate, Shorncliffe & Hythe Advertiser*, 15 January 1896.
13 *Ibid.*, 7 April 1894.
14 *Ibid.*, 2 March 1895.
15 *Ibid.*, 29 June 1895.
16 *Ibid.*, 27 April 1895.
17 Diaries of General Sir Frederick Solly-Flood, unpublished private collection.
18 KHLC: H/U21/F6.
19 *Morning Post*, 14 May 1897.
20 *Folkestone Express, Sandgate, Shorncliffe & Hythe Advertiser*, 26 February 1896 and 12 June 1897.
21 *The Queen*, 25 April 1896.
22 *Folkestone Express, Sandgate, Shorncliffe & Hythe Advertiser*, 23 July 1892.
23 *Wisden Cricketers' Almanack*, 1953.
24 *Cricket*, 22 June 1893.
25 David Boorman, *Hythe Cricket Week, 1894–1939* (Horsham, 2016).
26 Rayner.
27 *Folkestone, Hythe, Sandgate & Cheriton Herald*, 22 June 1895.
28 Rayner.
29 Boorman, p.23.
30 *Folkestone Express, Sandgate, Shorncliffe & Hythe Advertiser*, 24 October 1894.
31 *Ibid.*, 1 May 1897.
32 *Ibid.*, 20 December 1893 and *Whitstable Times and Herne Bay Herald*, 20 May 1899.

Chapter 14

1 KHLC: U3555/4/M/Bp5/6.
2 KHLC: U3555/4/Ba/1/1.
3 KHLC: U3555/4/M/Ba2/1.
4 Terence Lawson and David Killingray, *An Historical Atlas of Kent* (Andover: Phillimore, 2004), p.115.
5 *Ibid.*
6 *Folkestone, Hythe, Sandgate & Cheriton Herald*, 18 May 1912.
7 Rayner.
8 KHLC: U3555/4/M/Bp5/5.
9 *Folkestone, Hythe, Sandgate & Cheriton Herald*, 15 July 1905.
10 Unattributed ms, Hythe Library.
11 KHLC: N.B. Redman, *The Story of Milk Stout*, undated.
12 Quoted *The Licencee*, 5 June 1977.
13 *Illustrated Sporting and Dramatic News*, 19 February 1910.

14 *Eastern Counties' Times*, 15 April 1910.
15 *Southern Reporter*, 16 June 1910.
16 KHLC: U3555/4/M/Ba2/1.
17 *Ibid.*
18 *Folkestone, Hythe, Sandgate & Cheriton Herald*, 4 September 1915.
19 *Ibid.*, 16 March 1916.
20 *Ibid.*, 23 April 1916.
21 *Ibid.*, 27 May 1916.
22 *Ibid.*, 3 June 1916.
23 *Ibid.*, 13 February 1915.
24 *Ibid.*, 20 January 1917.
25 *Ibid.*, 8 December 1917.
26 KHLC: U3555/4/M/Ba2/1.
27 *Folkestone, Hythe, Sandgate & Cheriton Herald*, 8 January 1916.
28 *Truth*, 15 May 1918.
29 Lawson and Killingray, p.116.
30 H.L. Malchow, *Gentleman Capitalists: The Social and Political World of the Victorian Businessman* (Stanford: Stanford University Press, 1992).
31 *Folkestone, Hythe, Sandgate & Cheriton Herald*, 15 April 1933.

Chapter 15

1 *Louth Standard*, 28 April 1945.
2 *Kentish Express*, 22 June 1945.
3 *Folkestone, Hythe, Sandgate & Cheriton Herald*, 5 May 1945.
4 *Ibid.*, 28 July 1945.
5 *Ibid.*, 24 February 1950.